# Praise for *Arianism Revisited*

Students of the imbroglio known as the Arian controversy will be glad to have this lucid, comprehensive, and dispassionate survey of the diverse opinions that Christians of the fourth century held concerning the relation of God the Son to God the Father. The authors do not lose sight of the political and pragmatic factors which influenced theological formulations, and they offer shrewd reflections on the strengths and weaknesses of the party labels which have been devised to guide Christians through the intellectual hubbub of this era. The chapters on Gothic theology and the doctrine of the Holy Spirit ensure that this compact volume will serve the needs of both students and researchers more fully than any other history of the Council of Nicaea and its aftermath.

—Mark Edwards, professor of early Christian studies, Oxford University

This book provides a good, concise summary of the heresies known as "Arianism." It offers a helpful overview of the lines of development of the other, "heretical" side and is particularly recommended for students to read. Fortunately, later debates about the Holy Spirit and corresponding Latin and Gothic sources are integrated in a fitting manner.

—Uta Heil, professor of church history, University of Vienna

Armed with the gifts of scholarly precision and dispassion, the authors offer us the best single treatment of fourth-century Arian theology in its various forms. The reader meets formidable learning expertly distilled and delicately worn. *Arianism Revisited* is a model of lucid, even-keeled scholarship that deserves to be required reading for scholar and student alike.

—Alexis Torrance, Archbishop Demetrios Associate Professor of Byzantine Theology, University of Notre Dame

This text is a very welcome addition to literature concerned with that pivotal period in the development of Christian thought—the fourth century. The authors provide a reliable, clear, and up-to-date introduction to the theologies of those who did *not* embrace the Nicene Creed and the interpretations of that text that formed the basis of later Christian orthodoxy. There is nothing currently in print that accomplishes this task so elegantly.

—Lewis Ayres, professor of Catholic and historical theology,
Durham University, and McDonald Agape Distinguished
Chair in Early Christian Theology, Pontifical
University of St. Thomas (Angelicum)

# ARIANISM REVISITED

# ARIANISM REVISITED

## AN INTRODUCTION TO NON-NICENE THEOLOGIES

BRENDAN WOLFE
MATTIAS GASSMAN
OLIVER LANGWORTHY

FORTRESS PRESS
Minneapolis

ARIANISM REVISITED
An Introduction to Non-Nicene Theologies



30 29 28 27 26 25 1 2 3 4 5 6 7 8 9

Library of Congress Cataloging-in-Publication Data

Names: Wolfe, B. N. (Brendan N.), author. | Gassman, Mattias Philip, author. | Langworthy, Oliver, author.
Title: Arianism revisited : an introduction to non-Nicene theologies / Brendan Wolfe, Mattias Gassman, Oliver Langworthy.
Description: Minneapolis : Fortress Press, [2025] | Includes bibliographical references and index.
Identifiers: LCCN 2024042404 (print) | LCCN 2024042405 (ebook) | ISBN 9798889833857 (paperback) | ISBN 9798889833864 (ebook)
Subjects: LCSH: Arianism.
Classification: LCC BT1350 .W65 2025 (print) | LCC BT1350 (ebook) | DDC 273/.4--dc23/eng/20250108
LC record available at https://lccn.loc.gov/2024042404
LC ebook record available at https://lccn.loc.gov/2024042405

Cover image: Arius. Arrius hereticus, woodcut illustration in Hartmann Schedel's Liber Chronicarum (Nuremberg Chronicle), 1493
Cover design: Josh Eller

Print ISBN: 979-8-8898-3385-7
eBook ISBN: 979-8-8898-3386-4

# CONTENTS

## Part IV
## Non-Nicene Thought After 381

# ACKNOWLEDGMENTS

We thank Thomas Clemmons, Mark DelCogliano, Uta Heil, and Adam Renberg for their comments on drafts, and Carey Newman for his editorial advice. For their comments on earlier versions of this research, we are also grateful to Mark Edwards, Peter Heather, Howard Jones, and Rowan Williams.

# NOTE ON SOURCES

Comprehensive narratives of the Arian controversy appear in the church histories of three fifth-century pro-Nicenes, Socrates (called Scholasticus), Sozomen, and Theodoret. A history by a radically anti-Nicene contemporary, Philostorgius, survives in Byzantine paraphrase. We will ordinarily cite each of these authors simply by name. Following routine scholarly practice, we cite most other works by author name and common Latin title.[1]

The three pro-Nicene church histories can all be found online in serviceable translations from the nineteenth-century Nicene and Post-Nicene Fathers series, as can many works of Eusebius of Caesarea, Athanasius, and Hilary of Poitiers. A translation of the main source for Philostorgius, an epitome by the Byzantine patriarch Photius, is likewise in the public domain.[2] For a full view of Philostorgius's fragments, consult the copiously annotated translation by Philip R. Amidon, *Philostorgius: Church History*, Writings from the Greco-Roman World 23 (Atlanta: Society of Biblical Literature, 2007).

Scholars of the Arian controversy frequently rely on documents relayed within other works. The standard collection, down to AD 333, is Hans-Georg Opitz, *Urkunden zur Geschichte des arianischen Streites*, first published in 1934. Now printed by De Gruyter (Berlin), it has been continued, in an ongoing series, *Dokumente zur Geschichte des arianischen Streites*, published since 2007 by Hanns Christof Brennecke and colleagues. We cite each document at first appearance, in any given chapter, as "*Urk.* X" or "*Dok.* X," and signal the intermediary source(s) (usually limiting ourselves, however, to those in the document's original language). Afterward, we cite simply by *Urk.* or *Dok.* number.

The intermediary sources are regularly works of the fifth-century church historians, Eusebius, Athanasius (especially his *De synodis* [*On the Councils*]), or the *De synodis* of Hilary. Other common intermediaries include a Latin collection (the *Collectanea Antiariana Parisina*) derived from a lost anti-Arian history by Hilary and the *Panarion*, an encyclopedia of heresies by a pro-Nicene bishop writing in the 370s, Epiphanius of Salamis. These are most easily accessed through *Hilary of Poitiers: Conflicts of Conscience and Law in the Fourth-Century Church*, translated with introduction and notes by Lionel R. Wickham, Translated Texts for Historians 25 (Liverpool: Liverpool University Press, 1997), and *The Panarion of Epiphanius of Salamis, Book I (Sects 1–46)*, translated by Frank Williams, 2nd ed., Nag Hammadi and Manichaean Studies 63 (Leiden: Brill, 2009) and *The Panarion of Epiphanius of Salamis, Books II and III. De fide*, translated by Frank Williams, 2nd ed., Nag Hammadi and Manichaean Studies 79 (Leiden: Brill, 2013).

# TIMELINE

| | |
|---|---|
| ca. 320 (traditionally, 318) | Initial conflict between Arius and Alexander. |
| 325 | Council of Nicaea. |
| late 327 | Likeliest date for deposition of Eustathius of Antioch. Recall of Arius. |
| 328 | Athanasius ordained. Eusebius of Nicomedia, Theognis of Nicaea reinstated. |
| 334–35 | Council of Tyre. Athanasius condemned for violence and sacrilege. |
| 336 | Deposition of Marcellus. Death of Arius. |
| 341 | Council at Antioch. Wulfila ordained (if not earlier). Eusebius of Nicomedia dies. |
| 343 | Council of Serdica. West–East split deepens. |
| 346 | Ordination of Aëtius as deacon at Antioch. |
| 347/348 | Wulfila and other Christian Goths settle in Roman territory, south of the Danube. |
| 351 | Council of primarily Eastern bishops, held at Sirmium, condemns Photinus. |
| early/mid-350s | Athanasius publishes emphatic defense of Nicaea and the *homoousios.* |
| 357 | Meeting of the Western Eusebians, future Homoians, at Sirmium. Manifesto welcomed by supporters of Aëtius at Antioch. |

358 First Homoiousian synod, at Ancyra. Athanasius writes about the *Tropikoi.*

359 Signing of the "Dated Creed" at Sirmium, followed by councils at Rimini and Seleucia.

360 Council at Constantinople, led by Acacius and Eudoxius, results in exclusion of both Aëtius (already under imperial disfavor) and the leading Homoiousians

362 Julian allows exiled bishops to return. Eunomius and Aëtius begin ordaining bishops, without support from Eudoxius.

364 Homoiousian Council at Lampsacus.

364/365 Hilary fails to see Auxentius of Milan condemned for heresy. Basil's *Against Eunomius.*

366 Eunomius briefly exiled after usurpation of Procopius. Aëtius dies. Clash between Germinius of Sirmium and Valens and Ursacius.

370 Eudoxius dies. Demophilus of Beroea made (Homoian) bishop of Constantinople.

373 Athanasius dies.

376 Terving Goths cross the Danube. Euzoius dies. Dorotheus Homoian bishop of Antioch.

378 Goths crush Valens at Adrianople. Accession of Theodosius I.

380 Demophilus and Dorotheus deposed from bishoprics of Constantinople and Antioch.

381 Councils at Constantinople and Aquileia.

383 Council of the sects, held at Constantinople, leads to final exclusion of Homoian Arians, Eunomians, and Macedonians in the East. Wulfila dies.

| | |
|---|---|
| 385–86 | Conflict over the basilicas at Milan. |
| 386 | Death of Demophilus and transfer of Dorotheus to Constantinople. Outbreak of the Psathyrian schism within the local Homoian church, over God's Fatherhood. |
| 394 | Victory of Theodosius at the River Frigidus. A firm pro-Nicene is now sole emperor. |
| 396/397 | Eunomius dies. |
| early 400s | Encounter between Augustine and the Homoian official Pascentius. |
| ca. 419 | Augustine writes *Against the Sermon of the Arians.* |
| 419 | End of the Psathyrian controversy at Constantinople. |
| 427 | Augustine disputes with Maximinus at Carthage |
| 430s–40s | Historical works of Philostorgius, Socrates, Sozomen, and Theodoret. |
| 439 | Vandalic conquest of Carthage. |
| 484 | Persecutory edict of the Vandalic king Huneric against the African pro-Nicene churches. |
| ca. 500 | Composition of the Verona codex of Homoian texts, in Italy or perhaps North Africa. |
| 526 | Death of Theoderic the Ostrogoth. |
| 586 | Death of Leovigild, last Homoian king of the Visigoths. |
| 589 | Third council of Toledo formally converts the Visigoths to Nicene Christianity. |

# Introduction

As the first theological controversy within legalized Christianity, the disputes about the Trinity precipitated by the Alexandrian presbyter Arius have become normative in the church and the theological academy. When, in around AD 320, Arius objected to the content of his bishop Alexander's teaching, Christian religion was still largely contained within the Roman Empire. Imperial authorities' recent shift from persecution to toleration allowed Arius's and Alexander's epistolary appeals for support to convoke open discussion and meetings of church leaders; the further shift from toleration to promotion and partnership established an imperial interest in peace in the church, which gave the resulting councils and their decisions legal force.

The negotiation, over the following century, of the competing authority of theological argument, episcopal synods, and creedal formulae became the pattern both for resolving and for understanding doctrinal difference. The Council of Nicaea in 325 was the largest yet gathered and ruled against Arius and his supporters. It would ultimately prove authoritative, though only after decades of further debate. Its defenders associated with Arius's name all those who opposed their theology from a direction similar to his, whether or not those opponents avowed his influence.

This book is an attempt to provide scholars and students with a single, coherent account of the diverging and intersecting late antique theological traditions which have been called "Arian." The terms "Arian" and "Arianism" have been the objects of centuries of widespread use and decades of scholarly criticism. The natural analogy to terms such as "Thomism" or "Lutheranism" contributes to the false but widespread impression that Arius's authority was owned by others who taught the Son's subordination in being and glory to the Father, or that his writings established the parameters of a movement. The terms cannot be rehabilitated; and yet scholarship must take care not to overcorrect.

The research of recent decades has shown that the doctrine of the proponents of the equality of the Trinitarian persons, whether called Nicene, orthodox, or catholic, was not uniform or static. The Council of Nicaea was accepted by churchmen of various views, some of whom, as the years went by, were willing to draw on their moderate "Arian" opponents, while others were sufficiently extreme in other directions to be subsequently considered heretics. Among these "Nicenes" or "pro-Nicenes" (terms we use interchangeably), it is possible to trace out closer and looser theological and personal alignments over the years of the disputes. A developing and shifting alliance in favor of Nicaea, or rather a set of overlapping and sometimes conflicting alliances, drove ongoing clarification of the full implications of the genuine, *essential* equality between Father and Son, as asserted in the Nicene Creed of 325. The creed's formulations were not only received and propounded but revised and expanded at the Council of Constantinople in 381. The differentiated scholarly approach of recent years has deepened understanding of the late antique theological traditions that maintained Trinitarian equality.

In this book, we suggest that deeper historical understanding may be achieved by a similar approach to the traditions that rejected the Son's equality with the Father—an approach that recognizes diffusion and disjuncture but also influence and continuity among those traditions. In focusing on churchmen and systems of doctrine condemned as heretical by all major Christian denominations, we are not seeking to recommend them to the reader. We are seeking, instead, to provide an accessible, up-to-date historical overview for readers who may encounter "Arianism" in a wide array of contexts and with divergent denotations, but without a comparable strength of resources. While there are many introductory explanations of Arianism—whether legacy scholarship made newly accessible by being out of copyright and therefore free online, or modern denominational and popular presentations—these rarely take the results of modern research into account.

This research, which is voluminous, has revolutionized understanding of the events and positions of these fourth-century controversies. The order of events, which was nebulous and unclear, has been delineated into potential timelines. Polemical constructions, having dominated for more than a thousand years, have been unpicked and subordinated to close analysis of the contemporary evidence. The motivations of Arius, Eusebius of Nicomedia, Wulfila, and others the church receives as heretics, long caricatured as pure willful contrariness, have been sympathetically modeled as (flawed) defense of key points of revelation. We naturally cite key studies throughout, and an annotated list of further reading appears later in this volume, for any reader who wishes to explore further.

For two reasons, however, obtaining the best account of Arianism from any list of books would require reading thousands of pages: First, the standard references present histories of the controversies as a whole, so that heresy is only distinguished from orthodoxy, better evidence for which encourages lengthier exposition; and, second, traditions of interpretation have varied across different languages, such that a thorough learner might need to come up to speed on a different consensus in each of English, German, French, and Italian. Nor do all the primary sources central to this topic have translations, or even critical editions.

Our work will present the diverse range of individuals and alliances who propounded these traditions: people who fought with each other at least as often as with the defenders of the evolving Nicene position. Drawing upon recent decades' explosion of interest in finely parsing the divisions of the fourth century, it presents the major groups which fell under the label of "Arianism"—Arius himself, his "Eusebian" allies, the Homoiousians, the Homoians, the Heteroousians, and the Pneumatomachi—in close engagement with the primary literature. It also continues recent scholarly attempts to explain what those who denied the Nicene position affirmed in fact, rather than just in caricature, and situates their Trinitarian doctrines, so far as possible, within their overall theology.

The book does not canvass the entirety of the fourth-century disputes. Notably absent is any sustained treatment of pro-Nicene theology or theologians, whom we instead give the role of foil to the heretics, in an inversion of the customary presentation. They are a resource for understanding our topic (their opponents) but are not the subject of sustained reflection here. Nor do we attempt to move past late antiquity to other movements, which, after the extinction of the original traditions, have appropriated or been condemned with the label "Arian."

The one and a half millennia that separate us from contemporary writings on our subject, not to mention disinclination in intervening years to waste resources copying heretical texts (and sometimes their active suppression), have left the record of the theologies we are exploring unevenly thin. In many cases, our arguments, along with those of all scholars of the period, are to be understood as inferences to the best explanation, or even speculation on the basis of what remains. History and theology are inseparable in this type of investigation; we nonetheless take the opportunity presented by surviving texts or reliable reconstructions to step out of historical narrative. The overarching structure is determined largely by the chronology of churchmen, movements, and church-political events, but repeated snapshots of theological positions, built on the surviving non-Nicene texts, form the intellectual core of our work.

This book thus revisits "Arianism" in three senses: It explains to a general audience why the term has been deprecated in scholarship; it presents close scholarly rethinking of the ideas of many so-called "Arians"; and it points to the ongoing value to be obtained by retaining a sense of coherence among the opponents of Nicaea. That coherence exists in the first place on a conceptual level. The hard subordinationist claim that the Son is inferior in divinity to the Father, or the Spirit to the Son, unites the theological traditions discussed in this work. A strict subordinationism rests upon theological presuppositions, including characteristic exegetical moves, and brings with it certain logical entailments.[1] It therefore stakes out a definable conceptual space in Christian theology, one that will be shared (if only in part) by any theologies incorporating a similarly strong subordinationism. It is possible, therefore, to discern an underlying resemblance or set of characteristics shared by systems of doctrine, though diverse in historical origin and church-political positioning, that make a denial of the equality of Trinitarian persons a core dogma. Moreover, among the varying positions actually taken during late antiquity, there were concrete and not just conceptual continuities: Contacts including conscious influence do exist across the centuries of subordinationist thought, connecting late anti-Nicenes to early figures such as Arius or Eusebius of Nicomedia. "Arianism," when we are done, will still not seem an adequate historical term; but the continuities are salient enough to justify seeing Arius and many of the later non-Nicenes as exponents of broadly the same theological trajectory.

That trajectory developed over many years, and is rooted, like all Christian theologies of the post-apostolic era, in an understanding of scripture and of doctrines inherited from earlier in the history of the church. We therefore begin the first part of our narrative, on the formation of early "Arian" theology, with a succinct account (chapter 1) of the scriptural testimonies on God, Christ, and the Holy Spirit, the way they were generally read by early Christian writers, and the developing Trinitarian theology represented by Tertullian and Origen in the third century. Chapter 2 delves into Arius's own thinking, and the part concludes with a discussion of his defenders, the associates of Eusebius of Nicomedia, amid the church politics of the 320s through 340s.

Part II, likewise split into three chapters, unravels the complex theological developments of the late 350s, as the old Eusebian alliance split into three competing factions: those who drew ever closer to Nicaea in their thinking (the Homoiousians or, to use a traditional term, "Semi-Arians"); those who held a subordinationist theology while attempting to create compromise statements (often thought of as moderates and called Homoians in scholarship, but dubbed "Arians" by their ancient opponents); and those resolutely opposed to Nicaea while innovatively committed to the Father's knowability (the Heteroousians around Aëtius and Eunomius). These chapters are tied together by recurrent doctrinal concerns—in particular, the shared, ontological subordinationism of the Homoian leadership and the Heteroousians—and by a running account of the councils and meetings of 357–59.

The remaining two parts are shorter (two chapters each) and explore the development of non-Nicene thought against the backdrop of a resurgent and ultimately victorious Nicene Christianity. Part III concerns the span down to the early 380s. In chapter 7 we focus on a new theological battleground: the status of the Holy Spirit. We discuss positions, formulated across the Homoiousian, Homoian, and Eunomoian alliances, that opposed the Spirit's full equality. At the councils held at Constantinople in 381–83, such ideas were decisively excluded, and within a few years the coequal, consubstantial Trinity was upheld throughout the Roman Empire. That the new imperial legislation did not bring the complete marginalization of non-Nicene Christianity was a result, above all, of the spread of Homoian thinking among the Germanic-speaking peoples. Part III closes, therefore, with the theology formulated by Wulfila and fellow Gothic-speaking theologians in both Latin and Gothic (chapter 8). In part IV, in turn, we devote chapter 9 to later developments in Homoian doctrine: both practical theology (as evidenced by Latin sermons) and polemic against Nicene thought. The former is an important corrective to the common supposition that "Arians" cared only about Trinitarian matters; the latter, to modern tendencies to downplay the emphatically subordinationist strain in Homoian thought. We conclude (chapter 10) with a discussion of non-Nicene understanding of fourth-century church history—evidenced above all by the staunch Heteroousian Philostorgius—which shows up key elements of continuity both with Arius and his early allies and between the Homoians and the Heteroousian followers of Eunomius.

# Part I

# From the Beginning to the Eusebian Consensus in the East

CHAPTER 1

# Before Arius

## *God in the Scriptures and in Third-Century Theology*

ANCIENT TRINITARIAN THEOLOGY was a series of attempts to say who God really was. The participants in the Arian controversy wanted to glorify the being beyond all other beings, to make clear who it was who had created the universe, saved human beings from death, sin, and hell, and led his followers even now on the righteous path toward eternal life. Over the following chapters, we will explore the theological ideas advanced by those who ultimately lost out. Even in antiquity, the nuances of the available positions taxed less-adept churchmen. Now, they can seem mind-bendingly abstruse. It is essential, therefore, to keep the underlying issue squarely in view. The disputants frequently used terminology hard to translate between Greek and Latin, and even harder to render into English. It is easy, when studying Nicaea and its aftermath, to fixate too narrowly on these words, and especially on the formula "three *hypostases* in one *ousia*" (or "three persons in one *nature* or one *essence*"). That makes a debate about who God is into a debate about how to *talk* about or *describe* God—always a factor in theological dispute, yet not the heart of the matter.

The Arian controversy was not chiefly about the meaning of the words *ousia* and *hypostasis*. These were clearly differentiated only decades after Nicaea, did not make complete sense to intelligent Latin speakers, and were not expressly incorporated into the updated "Nicene" creed adopted, following the Council of Constantinople of 381, in both East and West.[1] To switch to Latin terms broadly equivalent to the Greek: The controversy did not hinge on the philosophical viability of a metaphysical concept of *substantia* quite unlike our physical "substances," or of *personae* that are not straightforwardly psychological "persons."[2] *Homoousios* (Latin *consubstantialis*, "of one being") was indeed a touchstone of pro-Nicene orthodoxy, but really only from the 350s onward. For two decades, Athanasius and his allies (few in the East, more in the West) had done largely without it. *Homoousios* was used by Latin writers, but they often expressed the underlying idea in a less technical language: Father, Son, and Holy Spirit were "equal."[3] That was the heart of the pro-Nicene view. From all eternity, Father, Son, and Holy Spirit were God to the same degree: a true Trinity in unity. With variations in East and West, that was the position that prevailed. It was a development rather than a simple restatement of Nicaea and the arguments then leveled against Arius. The alternative positions resulted in a very different view of the Trinity: a true and full God (the Father); a created, begotten, and subordinate God of all creation (the Son); and a created being, not God but above all other created beings, the illuminator of the human race (the Holy Spirit).

Amid all its complexities, therefore, the Arian controversy was, very simply, about who God is, and about how his Son—his Word, his Wisdom—relates to him. By about 370, what had begun as a controversy about Father and Son had become fully Trinitarian: How does the Holy Spirit, who is sent by the Son from the Father, relate to them? The controversy also involved disagreements, though they were normally less direct, over Christology: What does it mean for the Son of God to be "in the flesh"?

These questions are all scriptural questions. The Arian controversy was an extended series of interwoven debates about and from scripture. These questions are inseparable also from Christian practice and the hope of salvation. We can say this about the Arian controversy with fewer caveats than about the doctrinal disputes that dominate the history of Christian thought before the fourth century. In previous centuries, other claimants to the name "Christian" had challenged the unity of the Creator of the Old Testament with the Redeemer of the New Testament, had rejected the prophets or certain apostolic books, and had advanced new gospels and revelations. Everyone on all sides of this new controversy agreed that adherents of the old heresies ("Marcionites," "Valentinians," "Manichaeans," and so on) were out of bounds, and that any position that converged on theirs had to be heretical, too.

With few exceptions, the shape of Christian practice and the limits of the scriptures were not under dispute. They were givens, rather: data that everyone had to take into account when arguing for a particular way of viewing God, and realities that shaped each churchman's sense of his inherited confession. This was true even though the worldwide church had not developed a single, unified rite, codified an absolutely fixed canon of scriptures, or even promulgated a uniform creed. It was true because all the participants had received and agreed upon the basic parameters of Christian teaching as hammered out in the yet-more fundamental controversies of the second and third centuries. The Arian controversy did not mark a split between distinct religions with a genetic connection yet fundamentally different understandings of God (like the split, say, between Protestants and the Latter-Day Saints). Instead, it was a controversy *within* the Mediterranean-spanning network of Christian communities, led by local bishops, that Celsus, the late second-century pagan critic of Christianity, had already termed "the Great Church."[4]

Separate churches, distinguished by their Trinitarian beliefs, began to emerge in the 360s and took on fully distinct existence from the 380s onward (a process to be explored across chapters 6–10). None of them proposed significantly different configurations of the Bible, despite ongoing uncertainty over the authenticity of some books.[5] Even in liturgical and sacramental practice, variations among theological parties were uncommon enough that the few exceptions became notorious. Pro-Nicenes adopted the doxological formula "Glory to the Father and the Son and the Holy Spirit" in place of "Glory to the Father through the Son in the Holy Spirit." Some churches that belonged to a particularly radical branch of non-Nicene Christianity, the "Eunomians" or "Heteroousians" (chapter 6), used a single rather than three-fold baptism (apparently) "into Christ's death." In particular cities, at times of particular local conflict, both "Arians" and pro-Nicenes developed distinctive hymns, and different churches came to honor somewhat different configurations of saints, as their traditions diverged across the fourth century (chapter 9). All, however, still received the hallowed figures of the Old and New Testaments and of pre-Constantinian Christianity, and the vast bulk of ordinary practice remained consistent enough on all sides not to provoke accusations of innovation.

As a result, we can treat the Arian controversy as a debate about how to read scripture and think about God in terms continuous with later Christian spirituality and theology, in a way that is not possible when discussing many of the disputes originating in the previous centuries. *Their* scriptures are, so to speak, *our* scriptures—books any scholar or reading Christian would recognize as forming a plausible Christian canon. Everyone, moreover, acknowledged the underlying rule of faith, the understanding of who God is and what he has done, that arises from accepting the Old and New Testaments as genuine scripture. Creation is not a second-rate work of an imperfect deity. It is the preeminent display of divine power: what sets God apart from everything else. Redemption is not (as Marcion had held) the intervention of a higher God in the created order, but a work of the Son of God, by the will of his Father, the will of the same God who created all things. Christ's manifestation as man, finally, is not—*cannot* be—merely in seeming. It is a genuine entry of God into human flesh, to save human beings from everlasting death.

## God in the Scriptures

The Arian controversy arose, therefore, from underlying tensions within the scriptural account of the Father, the Son, and the Holy Spirit. We say "account," singular, because to all the disputants, the many books of the Old and New Testaments really did advance a single, unified teaching. Conservative Christian readers would still agree, but the way ancient churchmen thought about the Bible does not line up exactly onto any of those commonly used nowadays. Some ancient theologians were more literalist, others more given to allegory, but none had the archeological sensibility—the acute awareness of historical and cultural distance—that marks modern reading, be it "literal" or "critical," of the Old Testament in particular.[6] The result can seem, to modern eyes, a combination of the strictest fundamentalism, an absolute confidence in the divine truth of every word of scripture, with a shockingly free-wheeling impulse to trace contemporary devotional or theological preoccupations across all scriptures alike.

Ancient theologians did, in general, believe that the New Testament fully expresses realities only foreshadowed in the Old. They also commonly recognized differing emphases in the four gospels.[7] It would hardly make sense, however, to speak of their grasping "a theology" of Proverbs, or of Isaiah, or of John. The churchmen of the fourth century knew, in the very bones of their private reading and public preaching, that the God of Moses, David, Solomon, the prophets, and the apostles was the same one God of Abraham, Isaac, and Israel, the Father of Jesus Christ. Through his Spirit, he had inspired and directed the writing of all the scriptures. They had, therefore, to reckon with several realities patent in the Old Testament, taking utterly seriously wording that might seem to modern readers metaphorical or poetic—and without theorizing about what the passages might have meant "in the original context."

First, there is only one God. This was the teaching of Moses, the truth for which the prophets had been persecuted by idolaters, the truth for which martyrs had died, from the days of the Maccabees to the Great Persecution of 303–13. "Hear O Israel, the Lord our God is one Lord" (Deut 6:4).[8] They read in Greek (or in Latin versions resting on the Greek), which does not distinguish YHWH, the name of God, from *kurios*, "lord, master." Still, everyone knew that God, speaking from the burning bush, had declared his name to be *ho ōn*, "He Who Is" (Exod 3:14). God was the creator of the heavens and the earth "out of nothing" (as fourth-century Christians generally agreed—a key difference from Greek philosophers who held that God had shaped eternally existent matter). God was absolute being, before all other beings, and yet he is also the God who intervened, time and again, in the history of Israel, as recorded by the prophets and the historical books of the Old Testament.

Second, for many Christian readers, the Old Testament offers striking indications of multiplicity somehow alongside or within God. "Let *us* make man in *our* image and in our likeness," God says in Genesis 1:26.[9] The Lord manifests himself—with two others, apparently angels—to Abraham at Mamre (Gen 18). Someone identified with the one Lord God of the cosmos could therefore appear in physical form, and even eat. The same Lord rains down "fire from the Lord out of heaven" upon Sodom and Gomorrah—another sign that "Lord" (or "LORD," "He Who Is") could apply to a being present down here, face-to-face, with human beings, and not just to the invisible One God in heaven (Gen 19:24). The New Testament, of course, provides a solution to the puzzle, but the pattern was already clear from the Old Testament itself. A special representative of God repeatedly appears to the patriarchs, judges, and prophets. This is the Angel of the LORD. He performs divine actions—in Joshua, claiming the command over the "power" of the Lord of Hosts—has a "wondrous" name, is called "god," and appears to receive or mediate sacrifice, the primary form of Old Testament worship, to the Lord (Josh 5:14, Judg 13:16–22). That sets him decisively apart from ordinary angels, whose first action is regularly to redirect human worship from themselves to God. Other passages, though cast in quite different language, filled out the reality later to be revealed in the life and actions of Jesus. In Proverbs 8:22, Wisdom is "created" by God "as the beginning of his ways for his works"—she is, to use Paul's language about Christ, "the firstborn of all creation" (Col 1:15). In the passage from Proverbs, ancient Christians did not find merely poetical language. On the contrary, this was a direct window onto the most basic reality. Wisdom, identical with the "Word" of John 1, was the companion of God in the creation of the world. The power to create, the distinguishing prerogative of God, was shared by a being somehow distinct from him, yet so close to him as to be called, "Christ, the power of God and wisdom of God" (1 Cor 1:24).

Interpretation of the Old Testament was interwoven with interpretation of the New. Of course, the New Testament does not always proclaim the divinity of Christ directly. The proof is in Christ's actions.

He does the things only God can do: commanding the waves and winds, raising the dead, forgiving sins. His divinity is evident in his teaching, too, which he credits to direct divine authorization. What he sees the Father doing, he does; and whatever the Father does, he also does (John 5:19). These words are so familiar, to anyone who reads the Christian Bible, that their force can be lost. Ancient theologians—the "Arians" included—felt it in full. *Whatever* the Father does, the Son does also. This means that the Son is, in some sense, God: precisely what he allows to be said of himself by Thomas in John 20:28. He cannot be anything else—not if he does what the Father does; not if he really has received "all authority in heaven and on earth," the prerogative of the God who made heaven and earth.

The deity of the Son was manifest also from the actual practice of the church, which had always offered prayer and worship to Christ.[10] The martyrs had died for it, and no one was going to gainsay their witness. At the same time, three other biblical and devotional themes stand alongside the Son's deity and in tension with any easy explanation of his status:

First, both Old and New Testaments stress the invisibility and transcendence of God. He is not too lofty to involve himself with creation; but he still "dwells in unapproachable light, whom no human has seen or can see" (1 Tim 6:16). His "ways" are above human ways (Isa 55:8–9). Jesus, by contrast, is most distinctly visible: that, in fact, is the point! ("He who has seen me, has seen the Father," John 14:9.) Without entangling himself in human sin, he adopted all the other human parameters of living, even death itself. The Pauline letters heighten the paradox. Christ, who was "in the form of God," somehow set aside "equality with God," taking on "the form of a servant" and coming to be like humans (Phil 2:6–8). He was then exalted: back, it would seem, to a place he had already enjoyed; but what, exactly, is that place, in relation to his humanity or to the one whom Paul can call "the God and Father of the Lord Jesus" (2 Cor 11:31)?

Second, Jesus himself says, outright, what those passages could seem to imply: "The Father is greater than I" (John 14:28). The Father—in

Greek, often *ho theos*, "the God"—is somehow also *his* God. Jesus does not merely act like the Angel of the LORD, mediating the messages of God to human beings and receiving their worship. He sums up in himself a host of prophecies about Israel and the human race. He is "Son of God," a title used in Psalm 2:7 of the Davidic Messiah. He is also the "Son of Man" who approaches the throne of the Ancient of Days in Daniel 7. That is a title with divine implications. The Son of Man is worshipped and granted everlasting dominion (again, to ancient eyes, no metaphor but real, eternal, cosmic power without even a shadow of diminution or change). It underscores, however, what is evident in the gospels themselves. Jesus is also human. He is *the* man, the second Adam (Rom 5:12–15); but, however lofty his human status, he is not simply and straightforwardly absolute God, "He Who Is." He is subject, for a time, to human sufferings, physical limitations, and death, while still displaying the power of God to create and to forgive sins.

Finally, there is a third entity. In the Old Testament, God speaks often of his Spirit. Jesus himself warns against blaspheming this being as the gravest of all sins (Matt 12:31). He calls the Holy Spirit "another counsellor," implying a close similarity to himself, and literally or figuratively *breathes* the Holy Spirit onto the apostles (John 14:16, 20:22). Several Old Testament passages link the Spirit of God to creation. He (or *it*—the Greek is neuter) is present above the primordial waters in Genesis 1, and is sent, even now, by God to bring life to the animals (Ps 104:30 [103:30 LXX]). Paul says that the Spirit knows the "depths" of God (1 Cor 2:10). Already in the Old Testament, the Holy Spirit is linked especially to the life of faith and redemption (Ps 51:13 [50:13 LXX]), and Jesus appears, in John 14–17, to credit him primarily with a ministry of illumination, consolation, and judgment. That is precisely what the Holy Spirit is then seen doing, at Pentecost and in the impartation of charisms ("gifts of the Spirit") and the virtuous "fruits of the Spirit." Unlike Jesus, he is not called "God" in so many words; but, on the other hand, he has a singular "name" with the Father and the Son. This is not an abstract postulate, either. The "name of the Father and the Son and the Holy Spirit" (Matt 28:19) was and is the name into which Christians are baptized. In it, therefore, is the forgiveness of sins and eternal life. This is also the faith into which the Holy Spirit leads those who will be redeemed. The Holy Spirit's importance was therefore evident; but was he God and, if so, how was that to be understood?

## Setting the Boundaries

### *Third-Century Trinitarian Thought*

Intersecting with these biblical questions were convictions about the attributes of God—*what* he is—that ancient Christian theologians found within the scriptures, yet did not always straightforwardly develop out of them. They were not, of course, trying consciously to synthesize Greek philosophy with the Bible. Though they appealed to Greco-Roman parallels to defend their monotheism, Christian writers firmly upheld the uniqueness of their religion. They knew themselves to be answerable to the Bible and the church, not the theses of a fallible philosophical school.[11]

They were, however, still ancient people. Like us, they were shaped, even in ways beyond their own conscious understanding, by their cultural context. Inevitably, they answered theological questions that might not have been posed in quite the same terms by people outside their setting. Consider, by way of analogy, how modern readers of scripture struggle with issues of *freedom*, *slavery*, *nationality*, or (social? personal? economic?) *justice*. Social assumptions that past readers might have accepted without qualm are now for many people unthinkable. Modern political and intellectual concepts (often quite far removed from scriptural categories) simply *have* to be taken into account. With ancient ideas of God, something similar is often true. There was a shared vocabulary for and set of concepts about God, owed only in part to Greek philosophy yet definitely influenced by it, that helped to condition the Arian controversy and the debates that preceded it. The most famous of these terms are *hypostasis* and *ousia* in Greek—words implying individual or shared "existence," either one potentially equivalent to *substantia* in Latin—but they are by no means the only (nor necessarily the most important) concepts in play. No less significant are underlying presumptions about divine transcendence and supremacy over the material world.

These shared concepts do not reduce to a singular "Greek perspective." In the early third century, the preeminent Latin theologian Tertullian could hold that God, as spirit, is in some sense corporeal. That view was shaped by the Stoic conception of God as an all-pervading spiritual fire: exceptionally fine, but still strictly material.[12] However, the dominant philosophy of educated Roman people was shifting toward a revived Platonism. Platonist thought asserted a supreme deity, the immortality of the human soul, and the degrading effects of corporeal existence (summed up in Plato's dictum, "No God mixes with a human").[13] Against this backdrop, God's transcendence becomes sharply salient—and an acute theological problem. Doubly so, when the Jewish Middle Platonist Philo, a contemporary of Paul, had argued that the Word of God (the *Logos*, a title used by John) was intermediary between God and creation.[14] If absolute transcendence over material existence is a part of what it means to be God, then Christ might have (somehow) to be less fully God than his Father. Conversely, the fact that scripture shows God working through a "Son" and a "Spirit"—possibly, on this understanding, two attenuated levels of deity—could explain, as the concept of a Logos did for Philo, how the transcendent God can intervene in the world.

Hierarchy is, in fact, a key feature of the explanations presented by Tertullian in the Latin West and Origen in the Greek East for the scriptural witnesses about the Father, the Son, and the Holy Spirit. The trigger was a set of alternative theological accounts whose precise shape is now obscure. Church historians normally term this line of thinking "Monarchian modalism" or "Sabellianism," after its most famous proponent, Sabellius.[15] The opponents of this theological stream perceived it to declare that God was absolutely singular. "Father," "Son," and "Holy Spirit" were not distinct from one another. They were manifestations, presented across the history of salvation, of the same singular deity. Jesus Christ was God in absolute terms. However, since Jesus is a distinct character in the gospels and has human experiences that the Father does not, such teachings dissolved his own unity. As Tertullian explains his opponents' views, "Son" would denote Christ's flesh, "Father" his divine spirit.[16] The one agency of Jesus Christ, so clear in the biblical text, is divided in two.

In response, Tertullian and Origen developed subtle conceptions of the nature of God, which would preserve both the threeness (in Latin, *Trinitas*, in Greek, *Trias*) of the Father, the Son, and the Holy Spirit and the reality of divine monarchy. The Father is God preeminently. From him comes the Son, analogous, as Tertullian explained, to a trunk from a root, a river from a fountain, or a ray of light from the sun.[17] These analogies helped to account for the Old Testament theophanies and for Christ's ability to suffer without involving the Father in his passion. The eye cannot endure the sun, but it can behold a ray of its light; and a river, when muddied, does not pollute its source (though Christ himself suffers as man, not divine Son).[18] The Son can be described as begotten, sent, and made—he is, after all, the Wisdom of Proverbs 8—and is therefore second to the Father who begat, sent, and made him. He is a "derivation and portion" of the Father's divine substance.[19] The Holy Spirit, who is sent by the Son from the Father, comes at a third "level" or "degree" (both possible renderings of the Latin *gradus*), like a fruit from a tree, a stream from a river, or a point from a ray of sunlight.[20] The entire Trinity has, however, a single substance, status (or "condition"), and power, and Tertullian freely describes the Son as "omnipotent," since he is the Son of the omnipotent God.[21]

In Tertullian's understanding, the Son was begotten—"generated"—"by proceeding from God."[22] His language was still redolent of the idea, articulated by earlier apologists, that the Word had somehow been contained within God and only come forth for the work of creation.[23] Writing a generation later, in Greek, Origen offered a different idea, which would prove essential for later Christian theology: the eternal generation of the Son. The Son was not begotten at any time, or even before all times. To assign him a beginning (other than the Father, who is the Beginning, the absolute First Principle of all things), would be to say that God had not always been Father. As a Son "by nature," he is begotten of the Father in unbroken eternity. Origen derides those who fail to attribute a distinct existence (*hypostasis*) to the Son and fail to assert that he possesses an essence (*ousia*) distinct from the Father.[24] *Ousia*-language is important to Origen insofar as he used it to distinguish his understanding of the Father and of the Son from that of Stoic-inflected accounts similar to Tertullian's. The essence of the Father transcends bodily existence, and so for Origen accounts of God as body must descend into farce.[25] God cannot be known according to his essence and the Son does not proceed nor is in any way from the essence of the Father.[26] Instead, the Son is the power and the wisdom of God, present with his Father in the beginning and before all things.[27]

Tertullian's and Origen's ideas were a more coherent account of the biblical witness and of day-to-day Christian belief in God than the modalist alternatives. Fourth-century theologians would owe much to them, not least the organizing vocabulary of "Trinity," "substance," "persons," "being," and "power." Neither, however, had completely resolved the relationship of the Son to the Father. After all, to compare him to the Sun's radiance could imply either that he is equal *or* that he is quite inferior to the Father. Each, moreover, had downplayed the status of the Holy Spirit, denying the creative power that earlier Christians had acknowledged.[28] Tertullian had also identified the "Spirit of God" that "came over" Mary as the Son himself.[29] Though Tertullian himself was acutely Trinitarian, and later Latin writers did speak of "Father, Son, and Holy Spirit," most Latin thought was, in practice, often binitarian rather than fully Trinitarian until the 360s.[30] Once the issue was foregrounded, at around that time, non-Nicenes, both Greek and Latin, would deny the deity of the Holy Spirit entirely. Origen and Tertullian had provided a starting framework and key terms, while their opposition to modalism helped to fence off a range of potential theologies as unacceptable for Christians. However, it was still possible to take starkly differing interpretations of what mattered, within the rule of faith that they had helped to make more articulate: interpretations that would explode, sometime around 320, into the most sustained Christian debate over theology that had yet been seen.

CHAPTER 2

# Arius

About 320, an aging presbyter in the church of Alexandria, the pastor of a local parish church, became concerned that his bishop was teaching heterodox ideas on the Trinity. About his earlier life we hear little, but he was later known for his logical acuity and credited his doctrine to the teachings of wise, "god-taught" men.[1] He thus embodied an old Alexandrian model of theological authority: the expert teacher, pursuing truth about God to unusual depth. That fit well with the old model of Alexandrian churchly hierarchy, which made the bishop a first among almost-equal presbyters. When the bishop, Alexander, described the relationship of the Son to the Father in terms that sounded disturbingly close to Sabellian modalism, it was therefore natural for Arius, a ranking subordinate and a trained theologian, to speak up.[2]

The result could easily have been a passing disturbance limited to the Alexandrian church. Two lines of contingent events converged to make it much more than that. Alexander expelled Arius and his supporters, they fled to Palestine, and both bishop and presbyter sought allies among churchmen favorable to their theological outlook. Arius found them in several Eastern bishops, including Eusebius of Caesarea, the foremost Christian scholar of the day, and Eusebius of Nicomedia, the greatest ecclesiastical politician of their generation. In the background came a momentous political change. Constantine defeated his eastern rival Licinius, and so consolidated the entire empire under the rule of an unbaptized but committed lay Christian who wanted to establish doctrinal unity throughout the church.[3] Thus, the dispute between Arius and Alexander embroiled the leading sees of the Greek-speaking East of the Mediterranean—and, after the death of the original protagonists, reshaped the teaching of the entire church.

One of the great achievements of the last forty years of Patristic scholarship has been to extricate Arius, the early fourth-century theologian, from "Arianism," the mass of theological positions, some widely accepted among his allies and their successors, some a product of their opponents' polemical extrapolations, that the Christian mainstream came to reject as heretical.[4] No later churchman is known to have named Arius as his teacher, and it would muddy historical understanding to present Arius as if he were the founder of a church, rather than one radical exponent of a theological trajectory with significant diversity from the beginning.[5] Due, however, to its radicalism, his thinking establishes a theological baseline. The dispute between Arius and Alexander reveals, in unusually stark terms, just what was at stake in the controversy. We will therefore devote this brief chapter to Arius himself, before looking outward, in the next chapter, to the men who first rallied to defend him, then pursued a policy of ecclesial consensus against the most ardent opponents of "Arianism": the churchmen called, by those opponents, the "Ariomaniacs" (*Areiomanitai*) or, more charitably, "those around Eusebius" of Nicomedia.

## The Teachings of Arius

### *The* Thalia *and the Letter to Alexander*

When Arius appears on the scene, he is already fighting for his ecclesial life. Three letters survive: an appeal to Eusebius of Nicomedia, seeking redress for his treatment by Alexander; a confession of faith by Arius and his allies, sent to conciliate Alexander; and a second confession written after Nicaea by Arius and his ally, the deacon Euzoius, to win over Constantine.[6] Each letter is shaped to the theological concerns of its addressee. This is most extreme in the case of the confession to Constantine, which is stripped of all theological distinctives. The other letters are more trenchant, but neither gives an unclouded window onto Arius's most controversial teachings. For those, our best source are the remnants of his one work, other than the letters, that ancient authors were able to name: a theological poem called the *Thalia* ("Banquet").

Sections of two polemics by Athanasius claim to preserve elements. In *Orations Against the Arians* 1.5–6 (late 330s), Athanasius's own interpretations are intermixed. Most of the key points, fortunately, are attested separately in *On the Councils* 15 (359), under the heading "Blasphemies of Arius."[7]

One conviction shapes everything Arius proclaims: the absolute, transcendent supremacy of the sole God.[8] To Arius's understanding, God is "ineffable to all," with "none equal or like or of the same glory" to himself. He stresses God's uncaused existence: he is "without *arkhē*" (the word used in John 1 for "in the beginning," taken by Origen to refer to God himself as metaphysical origin of the Word).[9] By consequence, the Son, who has God as his beginning, must be fundamentally different from the Father: "The beginningless one put the Son as beginning of the things that have an origin." He speaks of the Son's having "nothing proper to God," being neither equal to him nor of the same substance (*homoousios*) with him. "The Father is foreign to the Son in essence (*ousia*)," and the Son, "being a strong god, hymns the mightier one in part." God's ineffability holds no exception for the Son. He, too, cannot fully proclaim the Father, and in fact does not even know his own essence (*ousia*). The Son "existed as Wisdom"—an allusion to Proverbs 8:22—"by the will of the wise God." Even as the primordial Wisdom, in other words, the Son is derived and extrinsic. Quite coherently, therefore, does Arius say that the "Trinity (*trias*) is of glories not alike"; their "existences (*hypostases*) are unmixed with one another," with "One" being "infinitely more glorious" than the others. "When the Son was not, the Father is God."

Arius accepts "myriads" of biblical ways of conceiving of the Son: not just Wisdom, but spirit, power, glory of God, true image, and Word; also "radiance and light." In a compressed set of lines, he says that "the mightier one is able to beget one equal to the Son," that he cannot beget "one more excellent, either mightier or greater," and that "the Son is as old and as great as he is by the will of God." The point, it would seem, is that the Son is the greatest of all possible created beings, yet not inherently unique. There could be another Son. Does this mean that he was *selected* for Sonship? Both Alexander and Athanasius consistently claim that Arius's Christ was, in principle, capable of moral change. Alexander says that "they" affirmed this orally, under examination,[10] while Athanasius, in the *Thalia* section from *Against the Arians* 1.5, has Arius explicitly credit the Son's exaltation to divinity to God's foreknowledge of his virtue. That is clearly a paraphrase, however, and secure evidence from Arius himself is weak—just the ambiguous statement, recorded in *On the Councils* 15, that God "made him Son" (a form of *teknopoieō*, which can refer both to begetting and to adoption). Moreover, in the letters to Eusebius of Nicomedia and to Alexander, Arius expressly affirmed the Son's immutability.[11] Perhaps, as Rowan Williams has suggested, Arius thought the Son technically mutable, yet preserved in his perfection by a continuous act of his will.[12] Something like it was not completely unthinkable, granted that roughly the same doctrine is later attributed to a radically subordinationist bishop of the 360s.[13] In Arius's case, however, we may just be dealing with a polemical inference by Alexander, perhaps encouraged by an unguarded statement from a local ally of Arius and later attributed by Athanasius not just to Arius, but also to his influential backer, Eusebius of Nicomedia.[14]

The shaky transmission of the *Thalia* leaves blurry the metaphysics of Arius's Son. No clearer is the impact of this complex of doctrines on practical spirituality. A few lines do imply a liturgical context and hint at a soteriological dimension. Arius says that "we speak of him, the unbegotten, because of the begotten nature; we hymn this beginningless one because of the one having a beginning; we revere him as eternal because of the one who has come to be in time." It is clear, therefore, that what knowledge humans have of God comes through the Son, and that Christians worship the Father through the Son's mediatory ministry—exactly what was implied when Christian congregations sang, "Glory to the Father through the Son in the Holy Spirit." Beyond that, Arius is not known to have said anything about the manner or purpose of the incarnation, let alone to have explained what the final ineffability of God, even to the Son himself, would imply for the possibility of salvation.[15] His concern, on the contrary, was to keep clear God's eternal superiority over all other beings, even the One who has brought us all we know about God.

## Placing Arius

In his letter to Alexander, Arius rejects several acknowledged heretics: the Gnostic Valentinus, who taught that the Son was an emanation of the Father; the dualist Mani, who considered him to be a "consubstantial part" of the Father; Sabellius, who in "cleaving the Monad" proclaimed a "Son-Father"; and the Egyptian ascetic Hieracas, who spoke of a "lamp from a lamp" or a "torch" being divided "into two."[16] Arius therefore sets his own theology against a web of second- and third-century positions, and sets those positions in his terminological framework, as well. *Homoousios* was on his view indicative of a belief that God was literally, even *physically*, divided into multiple beings. Sabellius's error was not, as it might seem to modern eyes, simply making Father and Son aspects of an indivisible God; it was proposing that a rupture occurred in the absolute "Singularity" (as we might now render *monas*) that was God. As Arius said in the *Thalia*, "The Monad was, but the Dyad was not, before he [i.e., the Son] existed" (contemporary philosophical language, but less alien in a context where *Triad* meant *Trinity*).

In fact, all the positions to which Arius objects involve some kind of division within God. He protested to Eusebius of Nicomedia that Alexander was teaching that the Father and Son had always existed together, and that "the Son is out of God himself."[17] In that letter, he granted that his opponents had put it correctly: He did hold that the Son was "out of the things that are not" (in Latin, and so regularly in English theological discourse, *ex nihilo*).[18] To infer, as he says in the letter to Alexander, from biblical references to the Son's coming "out of the Father" that he is an emanation or consubstantial part would be to make God himself composite, divisible, changeable, and corporeal.[19]

Arius's position rests, therefore, on a sharp dichotomy. The Son must either be a created being, clearly separate from the Father, or else the Christian doctrine of God is invalid. Thus, though he affirms that the Son is "begotten," the fundamental relationship between Father and Son—between the wise God and the Wisdom he established as the beginning of things that have an origin—is one of creation, not begetting.

Here we touch upon a divide that, decades later, will still separate the fully developed pro- and anti-Nicene positions and which in popular representations of the Arian controversy is sometimes misconstrued: the way in which Arius and Alexander, or pro- and anti-Nicenes, thought about the deity of the Son and its relationship to the Father's deity. It is not quite true, for example, that Arius denied the Son's divinity. Like all the later non-Nicenes, he believed that the Son was God, but decidedly not in the same sense in which the Father was God. In his eyes, one might say that the Son was God; but the Father was GOD. To call Arius "anti-Trinitarian" or to say that he was a strict "monotheist" therefore begs the theological question. Both Arius and Alexander professed that God was one, and asserted the Christian belief in a Trinity (*trias*) of Father, Son, and Holy Spirit.[20] They simply disagreed about how to understand those teachings. To say that Arius was "subordinationist" is closer to the mark, but only if one has identified the way in which he understood subordination and the role it played in his theology.

Subordination or hierarchy within the Trinity is always in practice a matter of the subordination of the Son to the Father or of the Holy Spirit to the Father (and often also to the Son). There are good exegetical reasons for this: the Son's according of superiority to the Father (John 14:28, "my Father is greater than I") and the sending of the Spirit by the Son from the Father (Luke 24:49). Subordination can be posited, however, along a number of possible axes, which interact in complex ways.[21]

First, we may distinguish *ontological* subordination: the idea that the Son or Spirit is, by nature, less divine than the Father. That claim can be made, of course, without actually using quasi-philosophical terminology for "nature" or "essence," by predicating of the Son or Spirit a less complete deity, a beginning in time, powers inferior to the Father's (for example, the ability to sanctify or make creation better but not to create *ex nihilo*), or anything else that would make the Son or Spirit less truly God. Second, we may distinguish *etiological* subordination: the idea that the Father is causally prior to the Son or Holy Spirit. This certainly can imply ontological subordination (for example, if the Son is held to be a created being) but need not (if, for example, he is held to be eternally begotten of a Father who shares his entire essence and attributes with him). Third, we may distinguish *axiological* subordination: according a primacy of glory. Here, again, one can distinguish extremes. Anglicans profess the coequal Trinity; but, per the *Book of Common Prayer*, they also direct public prayer to the Father preeminently. Some ancient non-Nicenes, by contrast, openly avowed that the Holy Spirit was not God: an explicit, public denial of properly divine glory. Fourth, we have *economic* subordination, which limits the Son's subordination to the incarnation or indeed to his human nature, the *man* Jesus Christ and not the *Logos* as such.

Ontological subordination must imply etiological and axiological subordination, but this does not hold in reverse. Thus, post-Nicene orthodoxy is able to accept an etiological priority of the Father and an economic subordination of the Son, without suggestion of ontological inferiority. Some ancient pro-Nicenes also accepted a limited axiological subordination, tying the Father's supremacy to his status as Father. What they did not accept is the belief that these forms of subordination revealed, or arose out of, an underlying inferiority of the Son's (or the Spirit's) being, a sense in which they were not fully God. At the controversy's beginning, those distinctions, left murky by third-century thinkers such as Origen and Tertullian, had not yet been finely parsed. Alexander held that the Son was a "mediating nature" between the Father and creation.[22] Under the framework we have sketched, that is a mild expression of ontological subordination.[23] To recognize this is, however, to begin to show where Arius and Alexander differ.

For Arius, the ontological subordination of Son to Father is a crucial theological truth. It is a concrete fact of the Son's existence—his *hypostasis* or *ousia*—and must be clearly and forcefully articulated if one is going to pay due honor to the God who is mightier even than the "only-begotten God." To get the doctrine of God right, one *must* affirm the Son to be less than the Father: enough so, in fact, that we might better speak of ontological *inferiority* than of subordination (something that is also true for many later non-Nicenes). In Arius's teaching, the accent lies on creation and so on the *difference* between Father and Son (and, implicitly, the Holy Spirit). For Alexander, by contrast, the accent lies on begetting and so on the *likeness* and *unity* of Father and Son.

In each case, the view of the Son impacts on the theologian's view of the Father: inevitably, since "he is the image of the invisible God" (Col 1:15). For Arius, the Son is extrinsic to God. Fatherhood is not an eternal attribute, though the one called "Father" existed eternally before the Son.[24] Arius's Son is unique in degree, but potentially not in kind. There could be no greater created being: understandably, granted that the Son has both the power to create and the glory of revealing God to rational beings and receiving their worship.[25] For Alexander, by contrast, God is Father eternally. This conviction could be taken to imply that God was Father *necessarily*, and so to impose a constraint on God's freedom of action (he would not be able *not* to beget a Son). That apparent constraint may, in fact, get at a key motivation behind Arius's theology: a desire to assert the absolute freedom and sovereignty of God.[26] For Alexander, at any rate, as for Origen, the Son is intrinsic to the Father.[27] He is God's own Wisdom, Word, and Power.[28] To describe God, it is not enough simply to be taught by the Son; one must also describe who the Son is and how he relates to the Father in whose "bosom" he exists.[29]

## Conclusion

At key points, Arius can seem remarkably prescient. His insistence that the Son was not equal to the Father and that the three *hypostases* must be kept distinct points directly to the typical language used, in West and East respectively, to propound the eventual pro-Nicene solution to the challenges he had first posed. We should be careful, however, not to read that solution prematurely into the early decades of the controversy. Arius was an extreme and therefore clarifying proponent of a theological trajectory; but the trajectories still had many years to diverge. Similarly, Alexander does not yet have a worked-out doctrine of the Trinity satisfactory to a later theologian. He does see, however, that the Son must be genuinely *in* God and *like* the Father, in some properly essential way: in some way that makes the Son really like the Father without overthrowing the Father's Fatherhood, and that makes the Father truly Father without making the Son extrinsic to him. The way is open to the Nicene assertion of the Son's ontological equality with the Father. For Arius, by contrast—and, as we will soon see, for key early allies—difference and separation were critical dogmas. The Son had to be recognized as *inferior* to the Father, not merely *less* in some way peripheral to the church's doctrinal concerns.

CHAPTER 3

# The Eusebians

THOUGH NOW IN the minority, church historians who lump together Arius and the other "Arians" have a point. Arius really was part of a wider trajectory, what has variously been described as a theology of "unity of will," of "the 'One Unbegotten,'" and of multiple divine *hypostases*.[1] It simply was not centered on his own theological peculiarities. From the beginning, even committed allies did not endorse his most extreme inferences from the transcendence of the Father (a key reason why "Arian" and "Arianism" have fallen out of scholarly favor). Almost no one was prepared, for example, to say that the Son was created *ex nihilo*.[2] Arius, however, did find ready allies, especially among those associated with the exegete Lucian of Antioch, a martyr of the Tetrarchic persecution (303–13).[3] He praised Eusebius of Nicomedia as "truly a fellow-Lucianist": possibly an indication that he, too, was linked to Lucian; possibly a successful attempt to win his way into Eusebius's favor.[4] Through their letters, he and his allies were generating connections and hammering out both points of consensus and points of difference with the nascent "other side."

The correspondence of Eusebius of Nicomedia, the leading politician in the nascent alliance, and Eusebius of Caesarea, its foremost scholar, are especially revealing. Writing in support of Arius's letter to Alexander, Eusebius of Caesarea stresses that Arius has made it clear that the Son is *not like* the other created beings, yet holds that Arius must be right that the Father—"He Who Is," the Greek rendering of YHWH—begat a Son who previously was not. Anything else would lead to two fundamental beings.[5] In another letter, Eusebius asserted that the Father had existed before the Son. Otherwise, the Father would not be Father or the Son, Son; if they coexisted, they would both be unbegotten or begotten, and of equal honor.[6]

Eusebius of Nicomedia takes a subtly different view. To him, Arius emphasized his belief that the Son had truly come into existence; that he had a Beginning and the Father did not, and that he existed by the Father's will.[7] To Paulinus of Tyre, Eusebius of Nicomedia quoted Proverbs 8 to show that the Son is "created, founded, and begotten in essence (*ousia*) and immutable and ineffable nature and likeness to the one who has made him." Begottenness is not a basis for inferring either generation out of the Father's *ousia* or "sameness of nature," since other created beings are called "sons" of God in scripture (thus Isa 1:2, Deut 32:18, Job 38:28). "Nothing," in fact, "has come into existence out of the Father's essence, but all by his will." He declares that the Son, "is without a share in the unbegotten nature nor from his *ousia*, but, having come into existence entirely other in nature and power, has come into complete likeness of disposition and power to the one who made him."[8]

Despite their theological differences with each other and with Arius, both Eusebii were willing to support Arius publicly. In Arius's doctrines they found a few key threads to endorse: (1) the supremacy of the Father, as the sole Unbegotten (*agennētos*, a concept not firmly distinguished from *agenētos*, "Ingenerate/One Who Did Not Come Into Existence"); (2) the greater honor owed the Father, due to his primacy; (3) the distinctness of the Son, as of everything else, from the Father's being; and (4) the dependence of the Son for his existence on the Father's will, and not on a spontaneous, necessary, or eternal relationship.

## The Eusebians After Nicaea

These four ideas will weave, in varying emphasis and combinations, throughout the theologies we will retrace in this book. They form the core of the theological trajectory linking Arius, his early allies, and later opponents of Nicaea and of the unity and coequality of the Trinity, down into the sixth century. Those allies were already cast, as early as the mid-320s, as mere "Arians."[9] "Those around Eusebius," a label also used by Athanasius, is more accurate. Eusebius of Nicomedia was not simply the key supporter of Arius in the 320s and 330s. With their emphasis on the Father's will and the Son's likeness in power and disposition, but not in essence, his early letters also anticipate theologies developed in the 350s and after (chapters 6, 8). By that point, however, Nicaea and *homoousios* had become central points of contention. In the interim, quite a different situation prevailed.

Held in 325 under the auspices of Constantine himself, the Council of Nicaea had received almost universal acquiescence, without a consensus about the meaning or accuracy of its creed. Eusebius of Caesarea's uneasiness about the *homoousion* is palpable in the pastoral letter he sent to his congregation after the council.[10] Quite likely, the term had been adopted chiefly because it stood so firmly opposite Arius's theology.[11] A text quite different from the modern "Nicene Creed," the conciliar creed includes several condemnations targeted at Arius's views.[12] Thus, the council condemned all who said "there was when he was not," "he was not, before he was begotten," "he came to be *ex nihilo*," or that the Son was changeable or mutable. Other points are interwoven, which implicate a broader range of theologians. Thus the council condemns those who say that the Son was created, as well as that he was "from" (or "out of") a *hypostasis* or *ousia* (words not then clearly distinguished) other than the Father's. It affirms, on the contrary, that the Son was "begotten . . . from the *ousia* of the Father" and that he was "true God from true God."

On the theological spectrum stretching from Arius to Alexander, the positions meant to be acceptable clearly clustered near the latter. The council left many possible interpretations open nonetheless: everything from Eusebius of Caesarea's assimilation of the council's decision to his own views in his pastoral letter, on over to radical assertions of the unity of Father, Son, and Holy Spirit. What we find, over the ensuing quarter century, is a continuation of the church politics pursued at Nicaea, where controversial theological positions are advanced in concert with—almost *by means of*—attacks on particular churchmen.

At Nicaea, the main target had been Arius, enough so that, when Eusebius of Nicomedia and Theognis of Nicaea later communed some of his allies, Constantine sent them into exile.[13] To endorse Nicaea properly, one could not contradict its theological utterances outright; but one also had to accept the council's assessment of who was a proper theologian.

Over the following decade, Eusebius of Nicomedia and his allies clawed back influence. They succeeded only in part. Alexander was never willing to readmit Arius, and his successor Athanasius, who became bishop in 328, held the line just as strictly. The result, in 334–35, was the meeting of a council at Tyre, with imperial support, to investigate charges brought against Athanasius by the representatives of a schismatic Egyptian church, the so-called Melitians. A commission was dispatched to Egypt and found Athanasius guilty of violence and sacrilege.[14] Following the council, Arius himself was due—so Athanasius later claimed—to be admitted to communion in Constantinople. Instead, Arius died in the most spectacular way possible: while defecating.[15]

Painful and disgusting deaths (ideally, involving the privy members) had been taken for a sign of God's wrath since 2 Maccabees.[16] Exaggerated though the story may be,[17] it was yet another reason for Athanasius to denounce his opponents, one and all, as "Arians." Among our few contemporary sources, Athanasius's works are indispensable guides to the historical events and a major influence on the fifth-century church historians, too.[18] In his eyes, he was beset by a host of conspiratorial "Arian" enemies of orthodoxy. That view has sometimes been dismissed as mere polemical "construction,"[19] but it is not entirely devoid of truth. Prior to 335, a number of bishops had been forced out of their sees. A prominent example is Eustathius of Antioch. A firm opponent of Arius and his supporters, Eustathius attacked them for what he saw as a denial of a human soul in Christ—a very different critique from Athanasius's, and prescient of controversies arising decades later.[20] He may have had Eusebius of Caesarea in view, and Eusebius was certainly instrumental in his downfall.[21] Nonetheless, to infer a full-blown pro-Arian "conspiracy" would exaggerate the degree of coordination underlying distinct church-political maneuvers.[22]

It really is true, however, that Athanasius was being targeted by men opposed to Alexander's theology and closely linked with both Arius and Eusebius of Nicomedia.[23] Take the commission sent to investigate his actions. Macedonius of Mopsuestia is comparatively obscure. Theognis of Nicaea had been exiled with Eusebius of Nicomedia, Maris of Chalcedon had sided with them at Nicaea, and the young Valens of Mursa and Ursacius of Singidunum, who appear at Tyre as the first and virtually the only Western Eusebians, went on to a firmly anti-Nicene joint career in the 350s and 360s (chapter 5). The final member of the commission, Theodore of Heraclea, is the best attested, since hundreds of fragments of his commentaries on John and Matthew are preserved in Byzantine anthologies, as well as eight pages on John in Gothic translation (chapter 8). Unfortunately, the evidence is too vague to specify what, exactly, he held, beyond his opposition to Marcellus of Ancyra (to whom we will soon turn).[24] One cannot help but suspect, however, that, if the commission had found Athanasius innocent—unlikely, since his church really did persecute the Melitians[25]—they would have had to find some other ground on which to condemn him. Perhaps even doctrine!

The real problem, therefore, with the idea of a pro-Arian conspiracy is that it presumes that Eusebius of Nicomedia and his allies did not have the right to speak for the church. In the 330s, when Eusebius baptized Constantine himself and became bishop of Constantinople, that was by no means a settled question. Characterization of churchly politics is inseparable from the question of theological authority. To call "those around Eusebius" a "faction" implies their *factiousness*, that they were not legitimate churchmen but an incipient schism (a question quite distinct from calling them a "party," a more neutral characterization whose validity hinges on the degree of unity and coordination one thinks the word implies[26]). Historians have often preferred to treat orthodoxy as relative to the position of a particular theologian or council: something can be orthodox by the standard of Nicaea or of later consensus, but not be orthodox per se.[27] Needless to say, this is not how either Athanasius or his opponents saw the matter, and it is not how a modern theologian answerable to scripture and the testimony of past Christians need judge the truth, either. To understand what was happening in the 330s, however, we must set aside the dogmatic clarity of hindsight. Eusebius and his allies were indeed cooperating, coordinating, and manipulating imperial power. They were doing this, however, to reverse what they saw as a manifest injustice—the deposition of Arius—and to undermine dangerous enemies not just of their own power, but of the truth as they saw it.

## One Hypostasis or Three? Marcellus, the Westerners, and the Eusebian Councils

Foremost of those theological opponents was Marcellus, bishop of Ancyra. Like Eustathius of Antioch, he is a stark reminder that the aftermath of Nicaea did not simply pit Athanasius against subordinationist "Arians." His theology is also a sign that Arius's concern about divisions within God was not just shadowboxing against long-dead heretics. The details, however, are far from clear, since we depend on hostile quotations in two late works by Eusebius of Caesarea, *Against Marcellus* and *On Ecclesiastical Theology*.[28]

Marcellus was writing against Asterius the Sophist, a lay theologian, aligned with Eusebius of Nicomedia, who had influenced Arius's *Thalia*.[29] Asterius held that there were multiple powers of God—and that the Son was a created, lesser power. Marcellus rejected this idea utterly. If Eusebius can be trusted (and it is not always clear that he can be), his theology was a revival of third-century modalism.[30] Marcellus emphatically rejected any talk of multiple divine *hypostases*. The Word and Holy Spirit were not merely "proper" to God; they were united with him so perfectly as "Unity" or "Singularity" (*monas*) that, in their procession from the Father, their Unity could be said to "expand" into a Trinity.[31] Accordingly, Marcellus treated "Word" as the key designator for the preexistent divine person incarnated as the "Son," Jesus Christ. Against this theology, Eusebius asserted the real and distinct existence of the three *hypostases*. Though the Son has the Father as his beginning and so is not coequal with him in honor, he is nonetheless to be honored "right next" (*paraplēsiōs*) to the Father.[32] It remains unclear, however, whether Eusebius thought the Son eternally begotten, and he still places him at a level subordinate to the Father: The Son gives thanks, prays, and is obedient to the Father, "his God," the "only true God," whom "he confesses to be greater than himself."[33]

These formulations represent much the same theology as was accepted by some ninety Greek-speaking bishops at a council, held for the dedication of a basilica in Antioch, that proved the most influential to meet between 325 and 359. Four doctrinal statements are preserved from the Council of Antioch 341 and its aftermath. The second gives the fullest doctrinal exposition; influenced by Asterius, it was later associated (perhaps only in wishful hindsight) with the martyr Lucian of Antioch.[34] This, the so-called "Dedication Creed," quotes extensively from the Bible, and lays out in detail the characteristics and salvific actions of Father, Son, and Holy Spirit.[35] The bishops had already repudiated dependency on Arius in a letter (the so-called "first creed" of Antioch).[36] At the close of the Dedication Creed, they anathematize Arius's more extreme formulations, condemning, in terms basically consonant with Nicaea, anyone who places any span of time before the Son or who makes him a "created being," "offspring," or "work" on a level with all the rest. Just as vigorously, but without explicit anathemas, the creed excludes the whole of Marcellus's distinctive theology. Declaring Jesus Christ "only-begotten God, through whom are all things, the one begotten from the Father before the ages, God from God, whole from whole, only from only, perfect from perfect, king from king, lord from lord," the creed names him "unvarying image of the being (*ousia*) of deity and will and power and glory of the Father." It asserts, moreover, that Father, Son, and Holy Spirit are each truly and genuinely distinct. The names are not empty designators, but signify "the proper subsistence (*hypostasis*), ordering, and glory of each of those named, so that they are three in *hypostasis*, but one in harmony."

Central to this creed is *distinction*. Father, Son, and Holy Spirit are not one and the same. Indeed, they are expressly self-contained: "whole from whole." The divinity of the Son is clearly asserted; but its degree is far from clear. By comparison with Nicaea, it is less: the Son is "God from God," but the Dedication Creed remains silent on "very God from very God." The resulting picture is of an ordered, gradated, hierarchical Trinity. Father and Son are involved in creation; the Holy Spirit, only in illumination and salvation. Their unity involves a genuine resemblance of both being and power, at least in the case of Father and Son, but consists ultimately in the harmony of their action: phrasing less stark than what Eusebius of Nicomedia had written, years before, to Paulinus of Tyre, but still consonant with it.

Eusebius of Caesarea had died in 339, two years after Constantine. Eusebius of Nicomedia died in 341. The doctrine articulated at his last council and incorporated, shortly afterward, into the so-called "Fourth Creed" of Antioch would remain the centerpiece of theological action by his allies, men such as Theodore of Heraclea and Maris of Chalcedon in the East, Valens and Ursacius in the West, down to 351. During that decade, a churchman in disfavor could turn elsewhere for support. Though Constantius II backed Eusebius of Nicomedia's old allies, he did not rule over the Western half of the empire, which stood under the authority of his brother, Constans. Accordingly, Athanasius and Marcellus availed themselves of Constans and the Western bishops, including Julius of Rome.[37] An attempt at a general council, held at Serdica (modern Sofia, Bulgaria) in 343, split into two sparring meetings of (primarily) Western and (primarily) Eastern bishops.

A polemical statement of the Westerners' faith illustrates the real divide between the anti-Arian theologies of the 340s and both the Eusebian alternative and later pro-Nicene thought. The letter assails the Western Eusebians Valens and Ursacius for asserting multiple, divided *hypostases* of Father, Son, and Holy Spirit and (it alleges) for saying that "the Word and the Spirit" suffered during the incarnation.[38] That phrasing, which appears to take "Spirit" to refer, like "Word," to the divine, spiritual person of the Son, no doubt reflects the Spirit Christology of Tertullian—a clear indication of the Westerners' distance from the dominant Greek patterns of theological discourse.[39] A little later, the writers declare that there is "one *hypostasis*, which the Greeks themselves call *ousia*, of the Father, the Son, and the Holy Spirit." They assert that the Father and Son have never existed apart from one another.[40] "The Father is Father and the Son is Son of the Father," they affirm; but they also "confess that the Son is the Father's power . . . and that the Word is true God and Wisdom and Power." The Father is indeed "greater than the Son, not because of another *hypostasis* or a difference, but because the name Father is greater than that of the Son," and they utterly reject a unity in mere "harmony and agreement."[41]

The fact that the statement is extant in Greek makes its reasoning only murkier. By *hypostasis*, the Westerners appear to understand what Tertullian had called *substantia*,[42] and so to be taking Valens and Ursacius to be asserting three distinct *deities*. That potential implication is an obvious weakness in a theology that locates the unity of the Trinity merely in "harmony," but the Westerners' wording cannot, by the same token, have allayed concerns that they did not appreciate the real distinction among Father, Son, and especially Holy Spirit.[43] The council ended, unsurprisingly, in an impasse.

No greater success would be achieved before 351. By that time, the Easterners had a new opponent: Marcellus's student Photinus of Sirmium (in northern Serbia). They perceived Photinus to be saying that the Son only became distinct from the Father upon the incarnation and, indeed, that Christ was a "mere man" indwelt by the deity.[44] Everyone else seems to have agreed in that perception, and it is now impossible to judge whether that is what Photinus did mean. Like the Easterners at Serdica, the Council of Sirmium 351 reaffirmed the Fourth Creed of Antioch 341, to which it added numerous condemnations meant to rebut Photinus and Marcellus and affirm the real and distinct, though subordinate, deity of the Son.[45]

Over the following years, Marcellus's former supporters would begin to distance themselves from him.[46] Perhaps the sustained Eusebian effort had worked; surely, the experience with Photinus had also shown up weaknesses in Marcellus's formulations. Even more significant, however, was the death of Constans, during a failed usurpation in 350. The empire was again consolidated under the control of one man,

Constantius II, who had for many years supported the post-Eusebian theology dominant in the East. His efforts at producing true and lasting unity would not only lead, through their ultimate failure, to the eventual pro-Nicene settlement. They would also yield the divisions, arising out of the Eusebian alliance of the 340s, that would set the distinctly non-Nicene theologies that endured into the sixth century.

# Part II

# Non-Nicene Trajectories and the Homoian Ascendancy

CHAPTER 4

# The Homoiousians

IN THE LATE 350s, the Eusebian alliance came apart. In hindsight, its creeds had always represented an umbrella position: They excluded the most controversial formulations ("there was when he was not," Marcellus's apparent modalism, etc.), but allowed for a diversity of individual conclusions about what the Son's status as "unvarying image" of God might mean. Now, people who drew those distinct conclusions diverged openly. Some, commonly termed *Homoiousians* by modern scholars, used the language of "essence" (*ousia*) to accentuate the genuine likeness of Father and Son in all respects—in effect, converging toward the pro-Nicene position. Others, the *Heteroousians*, reasserted the sharp distinctness, even the outright unlikeness, of the Son, in his essence, to the Father and the Holy Spirit to the Son. The third set, now called *Homoians* but termed "Arians" by their Nicene opponents, tended toward a similar, but less rigorously stated, subordinationism, and set the then-recognized orthodoxy, through councils held, in both East and West, in 359 and 360.

To reflect these developments, our narrative must inevitably become more complicated. This is a direct result of the slipperiness of Homoian theology. That customary modern name suggests that its adherents ought to have been "similarists," committed on principle to the idea that the Son was "like" or "similar" (*homoios*) to the Father. In actual fact, those we term "Homoians"—at that point, just a few Eusebian-leaning Western bishops—started out, in 357, by articulating a firmly subordinationist position (one that was not, in any literal sense, "Homoian" at all, since the key term *homoios* was absent). Their manifesto, which proposed banning *homoousios* and *homoiousios*, found support from Heteroousian-leaning Eastern bishops, but kicked off open controversy with the Homoiousians. Then, in 359, the Western bishops adopted a literally "Homoian" position, settling on a vague creedal formulation that merely asserted the Son's "likeness" to the Father, while retaining a ban on *ousia*. With support from key Easterners, that creed won out. By the 380s, however, its most stalwart adherents were again advancing a brusquely subordinationist theology—one shaped by developments in pro-Nicene thought that had been driven by encounters with both Homoiousians and Heteroousians.

An account of Homoian theology prior to the 380s is thus an attempt to describe a moving target. It requires a working knowledge of Homoiousian and Heteroousian thinking alike, and yet, those ideas, too, were in fact articulated in concert with the Homoian rise to dominance. The events at Constantius's councils, and the victory of the Homoians, are nigh unintelligible before one grasps the competing theological options. Even worse, an influential branch of Homoiousian thinking rapidly develops, by the mid-360s, into a half compromise with Nicaea. The early Homoiousian statements are clear-cut, yet for many they will have been only a passing theological phase. Something similar could also be said about the theology of any one of the often-blurrier Homoian documents preserved from before ca. 381. By contrast, Heteroousian theology retained its basic shape, yet its adherents diverged, in theologically relevant ways, from the mainstream church across the span from 360 to the 380s. Each of the three alignments therefore requires a narrative of quite distinct shape from the rest, if we are going to arrive at an adequate description of its theological peculiarities. Those narratives must also reflect both the differing outcomes and the practical church-political interconnection of Constantius's Eastern and Western councils of 359–60.

There is simply no way to tease apart the tangle of primary documents and conciliar events that preserves both their chronological sequence and a coherent account of each non-Nicene theological option. We have chosen, therefore, to begin by briefly introducing the earliest extant Heteroousian thinking, which formed a powerful foil for the Homoiousians and shaped the Eastern reception of Homoian church politics, and then to explore Homoiousian theology, which is neatly articulated in two documents written in 358 and 359. Those are tasks for the present chapter. In chapter 5, we will turn to the Western Homoians, tracing the evidence for their thinking as late as 381, before circling back around, in chapter 6, to Eastern conciliar developments in 359–360 and a fuller description of Heteroousianism. During the period of Homoian supremacy (359 to the realignments of 378–83), we will then see the further development of Homoiousianism in debate over the status of the Holy Spirit (chapter 7), and the acceptance and full articulation of later Homoian subordinationism by the Gothic bishop Wulfila (chapter 8), whose transmission of Homoian Christianity to the Goths would profoundly shape its later history. The last two chapters, finally, will consider non-Nicene thought after the pro-Nicene victories of the 380s.

## Preliminaries

### *Aëtius and the Eastern Reception of the Homoian Manifesto*

Setting the Homoians aside is made the easier by the split theological experience of East and West. For Western pro-Nicenes, the Homoian "Arians" would be a primary and enduring enemy. Other theological factions did not coalesce.[1] In the East, by contrast, the subordinationist Homoian manifesto of 357 made its impact through its reception by rivals with clearer theological views. It was welcomed by its Greek supporters, and rejected by its Greek critics, alongside the ideas of a particularly radical Greek thinker: Aëtius, first of the Heteroousians.[2]

A Syrian, Aëtius was a goldsmith by trade. Tenacious in debate and logically exacting, he gained patronage—and a theological education, evidently—from old allies of Arius and Eusebius of Nicomedia.[3] To their ancient opponents, he and his followers were "Anomoians," believers in the Son's positive unlikeness to the Father. Modern scholars have sometimes termed them "Neo-Arians."[4] That label captures important realities: above all, the direct historical, human links from Aëtius back to Arius's early supporters, and their shared belief that the

Son was positively unlike the Father in essence. Aëtius differed, however, from Arius on an essential tenet. Arius had denied that the Father was known even to the Son. Aëtius believed, by contrast, that human logic could grasp the essence of the deity. One of his works survives intact. In a sequence of thirty-seven theses (the *Syntagmation*) written ca. 359, Aëtius defended his core beliefs.[5] In a preamble, he claims to expound "the mind"—that is, the content and intention—"of the Holy Scriptures." Until a concluding benediction, however, his theses are devoid of scriptural prooftexts.[6] Instead, they offer a clipped set of logical propositions and inferences, which tend toward one conclusion: God is "the Unbegotten" (*agennētos*, or perhaps "Ungenerated," *agenētos*: the words, as often, are not firmly distinct[7]). He is that which did not come into existence: "the Absolute," as some have suggested rendering it.[8] For Aëtius, we might say, adapting St. Anselm, that unbegottenness is that beyond which no greater can be conceived. Indeed, if "Unbegotten" were a human invention, humans would have improved over God's actual essence by coming up with it, and so actually be greater than God himself![9] Thus, to call God "unbegotten" is to describe his essence outright. Even "Father" is a secondary, limited term—an implication, not stated in the *Syntagmation*, that was dogma for later Heteroousians—while the Son, the Only-Begotten, is not properly "God."[10]

Aëtius's doctrines rested on a rational precision few will have been able to maintain. No wonder, then, that others claimed that he held Christ simply to be "unlike" the Father. However, he offered a more accurate description, which had by the 430s become his followers' watchword (chapter 10): Christ was "other in essence" (*heteroousios*) to the Father.[11] That term justifies the use of "Heteroousians" as a rare in-group designator for a church generally adjudged heretical. It also sets Aëtius's followers neatly at odds not just with pro-Nicenes, but also with the party that, for a brief span, was poised to set the accepted orthodoxy for the entire empire. These are the alliance of Eusebians whom scholars generally call "Homoiousians," proponents of the doctrine that the Son was genuinely "like the Father in all things," explicitly including "in essence."[12]

## The Synod of Ancyra 358 and the Homoiousian Manifesto

Few churchmen of antiquity have been done less justice, in popular imagining of the Arian controversy, than the Homoiousians. Their theological formulations were welcomed—with careful interpretation—by pro-Nicene champions East and West, as both Athanasius and an increasingly prominent Latin anti-Arian, Hilary of Poitiers, concluded that a logically consistent Homoiousian would embrace Nicaea.[13] However, pro-Nicene heresiologists, though still aware of potential rapprochement, fixated on their failure to embrace the full, consubstantial equality of Father and Son.[14] "Semi-Arians" they came to be called, and are sometimes confused nowadays with their Homoian opponents: a conflation of *homoios* and *homoiousios* hardly eased by Edward Gibbon's memorable, but misleading, quip about "the furious contests" aroused by the "single diphthong" separating *homoousios* and *homo**i**ousios*.[15]

To understand Homoiousian thinking, we have to get beyond both contemporary pro-Nicene interest in a potential alliance and the blinkers of later critics. Fortunately, we have an excellent basis for reconstructing their reasoning. Two documents are preserved by the pro-Nicene Epiphanius of Salamis in the entry on "Semi-Arians" in his encyclopedia of heresies (ca. 377). These give direct access to the arguments of the early Homoiousians. One is the text we will first examine: the letter, issued by a synod hosted at Ancyra by the bishop Basil in 358, that opposed the Heteroousian thinking of Eudoxius and Aëtius.[16] The second is a letter written in 359 by George, bishop of Laodicea, and approved by Basil, that clarified Homoiousian thinking after an uneasy rapprochement with the Homoians.[17]

Neither Basil nor George was a crypto-Nicene. Basil had been ordained to the see of Ancyra following the deposition of Marcellus. His career literally depended on his rejection of an extreme pro-Nicene position. George had a colorful ecclesial past.[18] When the controversy first broke out, he had been a presbyter at Alexandria, where he had simultaneously defended Arius's "there was when he was not" to

Alexander's partisans and Alexander's derivation of the Son from the Father to Arius's.[19] Persisting in communion with Arius, he had been excommunicated by Alexander.[20] Thus, he had not only maintained impolitic loyalties but also encouraged toleration—now frustratingly devoid of context—for one of Arius's most controversial ideas. By the mid-350s, however, Arius had been dead some two decades. George was an ally of Eusebius of Emesa (a student of Eusebius of Caesarea) and Cyril of Jerusalem. The sermons of both churchmen, still extant, reveal a relatively high view of the Son, coupled with staunch resistance to modalism.[21] This theology squares neatly with the ideas expressed, using the language of *ousia*, in the letters of the Homoiousians. The letter of the Ancyrene synod of 358 lays claim to the Eastern conciliar tradition, rejecting both Marcellian modalism and a new heresy: what the bishops allege to be a doctrinal alliance, blending those now termed Heteroousians and Homoians, that focuses on the inferiority and createdness of the Son.[22]

Sonship and Fatherhood are the central theme of the synodical letter. In theory, the bishops defend the entire Trinity, asserting the priority of the names "Father, Son, and Holy Spirit" from the baptismal formula of Matthew 28:19.[23] However, the Holy Spirit still plays a marginal role, as in preceding stages of the debate. The focus lies overwhelmingly on the Father and the Son. The authors do use philosophical language, arguing, for example, that "every father is considered the father of an *ousia* like him."[24] The core, however, is exegesis, not philosophy. What drives their doctrine is not inference from axioms about the deity, but the belief that "Father" and "Son" are the true, properly descriptive names for the divine persons. These names, which imply ontological likeness between the divine persons, must take precedent over other paired terms that imply ontological distinction: "Un-incarnate" and "Incarnate"; "Immortal" and "Mortal"; and "Unbegotten" and "Begotten."[25]

Basil and his allies do grant the language of "Creator" (*ktistēs*) and "Creature" (*ktisma*) to be biblical—which it is, by extrapolation from the Septuagint text of Proverbs 8:22—but reduce its Trinitarian significance to three features of creation that are not necessarily features of begetting: (1) that making occurs without suffering; (2) that the thing created is perfect (i.e., *finished* and *mature*, in Greek, *teleios*); and (3) that that which is made is made in accordance with the Creator's will.[26] The fear, however, of the ideas of making with *pathos* or by emanation—which they, too, reject—must not lead one to consider the Son merely another "work."[27] To take that step simply does not befit the relationship between Father and Son, and it is not enough to say that all things were in turn made through the Son, as that will reduce him simply to the first of creations and an instrument in creation.[28]

To back up their reasoning, the bishops must reckon with two ready objections, both of which hearken back to the beginning of the controversy. The first is the existence of biblical passages that refer to numerous, obviously created "sons" of God. These they dismiss as mere figures of speech.[29] The analogy to earthly fatherhood, made by Paul himself at Ephesians 3:14–15, is key. Fatherhood, properly defined, is of a Son like oneself. The second is the concern that their doctrine would require God to have "undergone suffering, division, or emanation"—in other words, that it leads straight back to the modalist position they have rejected.[30] Following Paul's appeal to the "foolishness" of God in 1 Corinthians 1:17–20, they refuse to explain the mystery of the Son's begetting, but deny that the begetting of Wisdom by "the wise God" can entail suffering.[31] They continue with interwoven close readings of key Old Testament (Prov 8) and New Testament texts (Col 1:15–16, John 1 and 5:19, 26) about the divine status of Christ.[32] Divine simplicity is the decisive premise: The Father is life "without compounding," and so the Son has (or *is*) life in like fashion.

Before a concluding barrage of anathemas against both Heteroousian and modalist thinking, Basil and his allies take another crucial step: They argue from the likeness between Father and Son that they are not "the same in all ways." The basis is again a close reading of a key biblical prooftext, now the Christological hymn in Philippians 2, together with Romans 8:3.[33] There, the language of "likeness" is expressly employed by Paul, in reference to Christ's humanity. This establishes both the likeness of Christ to the Father and a genuine difference. The incarnate Son both is and is not man, insofar as he lacks sins and was generated without passion. Thus also, he has the properties of the deity—likeness to the Father in deity, incorporeality, and actions—and yet is not the same as God: a distinction adumbrated, they say, in the lack of a definite article in the key phrases in Philippians 2:6 (being "in form of God" and laying aside "equality with God").

The letter of the synod of Ancyra is recognizably an initial position-statement, still hazy on the incarnation and divine relations. Logically imprecise, it can hardly have appealed to genuine supporters of Aëtius, but it did not need to. Opening with the Eusebian councils and concluding with an anathema against the *homoousion*—the sole reference to the pro-Nicene position, beyond Marcellus and Photinus—it was clearly meant to draw the support of Eastern bishops who respected the hallowed authority of Antioch 341. Likely, the bishops also hoped to win the backing of Constantius II, who had long been pushing for acceptance of the deposition of Marcellus and Athanasius.[34] If so, they succeeded. Homoiousian bishops went twice to the court of Constantius at Sirmium in northern Serbia. First, they gained the emperor's endorsement for the Dedication Creed of Antioch 341 and reiterated many of the condemnations they had made at Ancyra.[35] Then, in May 359, they met, at the emperor's invitation, to help formulate the creed that would be put before the councils slated to unite the church's confession throughout the empire.

## The Road to Rimini–Seleucia

The second Homoiousian manifesto, the letter of George of Laodicea, was written in the aftermath of the Sirmian meeting of 359. On its face, the meeting had been a qualified success for all concerned: emperor, Homoians, and Homoiousians. The bishops had endorsed a consensus creed advanced by the meeting president, Mark of Arethusa in Syria. Theologically colorless, the "Dated Creed" of May 22, 359, declared the Son to be "like the Father who begat him, according to the scriptures," and again, "like the Father in all things, as the scriptures say and teach."[36] It also forbade the term *ousia* on milder grounds than those preferred (as we will see in chapter 5) by the Homoians: It was not scriptural, and so tended to confuse the laity. Neither Homoians nor Homoiousians were content. According to an account George appended to his letter, the Homoian spokesman Valens tried to leave off "in all things" in his subscription to the creed, until Constantius II caught him out. Basil, for his part, did everything he could to accentuate the Son's ontological likeness to the Father: He was like "in all things, not just will, but *hypostasis*, existence, and being."[37] The battle lines were set, and George, with Basil's support, was now preparing for the contest.

Amid deep continuity of thought, this second manifesto makes a series of striking developments over the first. At Sirmium in 358, Basil had rejected the *homoousion* on theological, traditional, and scriptural grounds.[38] The new manifesto, which maintains the attack on Marcellus, does not retract this hostility toward the Nicene formula. It does not reiterate it, either. It also takes several important steps. First, it directly defends the use of *ousia* as an extrapolation from the biblical name of God (YHWH, in Greek *ho ōn*, "He who is").[39] Second, it makes even clearer that the Homoiousians' opponents are inspired both by the Homoians and by Aëtius: They are believers in the unlikeness of the Son to the Father, critics of the term *ousia*, and readers of the 357 Sirmian manifesto.[40] Third, George acknowledges that his opponents do admit the likeness of the Son to the Father "only in will" and "in activity."[41] A Heteroousian objection to the label "Anomoian"—one voiced also by later Homoians when accused of holding the Son to be unlike the Father—is therefore anticipated.[42] The question is not whether the Son is in some degree like the Father. It is whether he is like the Father in what he *is*, rather than what he *does*.

Fourth, the manifesto finally lays out a properly Trinitarian theology. Defending the term *hypostasis*, George explains that it denotes the "subsistent and existing properties of the persons."[43] This does not lead to three Gods, or for that matter to two Gods, but to belief in "one deity that encompasses all things through the Son in the Holy

Spirit." This Trinity is still hierarchical, originating from a Father who "subsists in paternal sovereignty," and attention soon collapses back onto the Father–Son distinction. The Homoiousians are, by modern standards, subordinationist—concerned, that is, to assert the Father's supreme sovereignty without also affirming ontological equality as the post-Nicene consensus would require. They also do not affirm the Spirit's deity as such. Neither, however, do they assert a positive difference in grade or quality of being between Father and Son or even between Son and Holy Spirit. They hold dogmatically to the supremacy of the Father, not to the inferiority of the Son and the Holy Spirit.

This doctrine leads to the last and most striking development over the previous manifesto. Revisiting Philippians 2 and Romans 8:3, George lays out broadly the same doctrine as he and his colleagues had adopted at Ancyra in 358. The terms, however, have been flipped. Rather than say that Christ is both man and not man, and "God the Son before the ages" and "not the same thing as God," George (and Basil, with him) state that Christ is, in respect to his divine spirit, "the same thing as God," and yet, in view of the incarnation, "like the Father and not the same as the Father"—just, in fact, as he is both the same as and yet "in the likeness" of human beings.[44] This, in turn, leads them to a clearer statement of what is at stake in the reservation of "sovereignty" to the Father. Passages such as Romans 8:3 and John 5:19 explain the likeness of the Son to the Father in will and action (still a doctrine the Homoiousians wish to defend, though insufficient without the likeness in *ousia*). The Father acts "in sovereign fashion," the Son "in a servant's fashion."[45] Although the Son's subordinate activity is still linked to his divine person and not the incarnation—the preferred solution of many pro-Nicenes—it is not a proof of his inferiority, but of his true likeness to the Father, whose actions he imitates (John 5:19).

## Conclusion

George's defense of the thinking of "the Easterners" on *hypostases* implies that he was writing (at least in part) to warn Western readers of the alliance between Homoian and Heteroousian churchmen developing in the East.[46] The statement is, on one level, a clarification of the Homoiousians' real position, which had been muddied by the grudging compromise at Sirmium that May.[47] It must also be a practical piece of church politics, seeking to build support among Latin speakers who rejected a hard subordination of Son to Father but held residual suspicions about the wider Eastern tradition back to Antioch 341. George avoids a direct attack on the Western Homoian leaders, stressing the use of the Sirmian manifesto by his Eastern opponents, and suggests that a meeting at Sirmium (presumably in 358) had refuted the heretical opinion of the Son's unlikeness in essence.[48] He also makes a revealing assertion: The heretics had been resisted by the emperor himself.[49] Despite the compromise in May 359, the Homoiousian leadership is still hopeful of both Western support and imperial backing. Both, as we will see, proved unreliable, and the Homoiousian alliance would be decisively excluded from the settlement of 359–360.

CHAPTER 5

# The Western Homoians

OFTEN, TO TRACE out trajectories within non-Nicene thought is to discern a theological motivation behind maneuverings at councils and pro-Nicene polemical extrapolations. Among the doctrinal streams that coalesced in the late 350s, this is most true of those whom scholars have dubbed "Homoians." This alliance set the recognized orthodoxy (especially in the East) until the 380s, and thereafter made up minority "Arian" churches (especially in the West) down to the conversion of the Visigoths to pro-Nicene Christianity in 589. Their views are much harder to grasp than those of their rival parties. In Aëtius, Basil of Ancyra, and George of Laodicea, we have recognized leaders whose doctrinal statements show how they "did theology." We can also select neutral labels that neatly replace the polemical "Anomoians" and "Semi-Arians." Terms used by members of each party encapsulate their distinctive positions, parallel to the Nicene *homoousion*: The Son is "other in essence" (*heteroousios*) or "like in essence" (*homoios kat'ousian*; later, *homoiousios*) to the Father.

With the Homoians, we are in a more difficult position. Pro-Nicenes called them "Arians," but, true to their Eusebian roots, they rejected Arius's most distinctive doctrines. The label does point, however, to a key characteristic of an otherwise slippery grouping. Tied to councils held in 359–360, their creed rejected all formulations built around "essence" (*ousia*), in favor of stating that Christ was simply "like" (*homoios*) to the Father. Over time, however, the weight of the Homoian polemic was turned against the Nicenes specifically. The Homoians were not strictly "Arians," and they may not have started out exclusively as anti-Nicenes, but anti-Nicenes is what they became.[1]

The appearance of *homoios*, "like, similar, alike," in this distinctive creed is the basis for the term "Homoian": a modern invention parallel with Homoousian, Homoiousian, and Heteroousian. The resemblance is superficial. The Homoian creed was first formulated through a short-lived, tactical compromise between Homoiousian leaders and those Eusebians, former colleagues of theirs, who prevailed at the Western council of 359. "Homoian" is an accurate term for the creed of 359–360 and, due to its theological and geographical neutrality, the best label for those, in both East and West, who held to that creed in opposition to Nicaea. It is, however, a term of convenience, which does not adequately describe the theology of this set of Eusebians.

To get at that theology we do not, unfortunately, have an early statement anywhere near so thorough as those of Basil, George, or Aëtius. In fact, we cannot even be sure how wide an alliance of "Homoians" really did follow the theological promptings of their churchly leadership. The settlement reached in 359–360 included bishops who certainly sympathized with Aëtius but condemned him anyway; others (in the West) who had vociferously backed Nicaea a few months before; and yet others (in the East) who had lately affirmed their support for Antioch 341. The Homoians had not hammered out what mattered, what did not, and where alternative formulations could be accepted. Rather, their creed papered over genuine differences, while leaving churchly power in the hands of a few particularly adroit bishops, who later tried to rule out formulations that advanced what they felt to be too high a view of the Son.

Under these circumstances, the only possible way to understand Homoian thinking is to begin in the 350s and work our way through to the 380s. Our focus is on theology, so we will dwell primarily on the Western Homoians.[2] It was among the small cadre of Latin-speaking Eusebians that the Homoian approach to theology began; it is among the Westerners, two decades later, that we can begin to see what had changed since the late 350s; and it is among the Westerners, therefore, that we can trace out a few of the enduring patterns of thought that gave rise to the longest-lived form of non-Nicene Christianity. Chief among these, as we will see, is not a principled objection to non-biblical language or a belief in the positive "likeness" of Son to Father, but the Son's complete subordination.

## The Sirmian Manifesto of 357

In 357, a small group of bishops met at Sirmium, at the behest of Constantius II, to frame a position paper that would help guide the world's bishops to theological unity.[3] We can name five attendees: Potamius, bishop of Lisbon; the elderly Ossius of Cordoba, alleged architect of the Nicene Creed and a Western leader at Serdica in 343; Germinius, who had replaced the deposed Photinus as bishop of Sirmium; and the two Latin-speaking stalwarts of the Eusebian party, Valens of Mursa (Osijek, Croatia) and Ursacius of Singidunum (Belgrade). Though well-informed pro-Nicenes credited the writing of the position statement, at least in part, to Potamius and Ossius,[4] there is no doubt that Valens and Ursacius were the true architects of the manifesto, known to furious pro-Nicenes as the "Blasphemy of Sirmium."

More than any others, Valens and Ursacius would drive the acceptance of the Homoian creed. Members of the commission that had investigated Athanasius in 335 (chapter 3), they had been taught, so Athanasius once alleged, by Arius himself.[5] That was no doubt speculation, since Athanasius does not repeat the charge and none of their Western enemies took it up, but it was certainly plausible. Arius and his closest supporters had been exiled to their homeland, Illyricum—the Danube frontier region—which became the heartland of Latin Homoianism.[6] Under pressure in the 340s, Valens and Ursacius had temporarily rescinded their objections to Athanasius and reiterated their rejection (in keeping with Eusebian councils back to Antioch 341) of "Arian heresy."[7] At Sirmium in 351, they were firmly back on the Eusebian side and, at ensuing Western councils, had spearheaded the expulsion of bishops reluctant to accept the condemnation of Athanasius.[8] Now, finally, they set out their doctrinal agenda.

Valens and Ursacius are bluntly subordinationist. After a preamble, their statement begins: "It is agreed that there is one God, omnipotent and Father, just as is believed throughout the entire world, and his unique son, Jesus Christ, the Lord our Savior, begotten from him before the ages; but there cannot be two gods, nor ought they be proclaimed."[9] Quoting John 20:17 and Romans 3:29–30, the bishops drive home this fundamental monotheist conviction: "Therefore the God of all is one." Thus phrased, the implication is that only the Father is, in fact, God. Immediately thereafter, the bishops head off the philosophical flanking maneuver that could leave Christ still equal (or nearly so) to the Father. *Substantia*, "what in Greek is called *ousia* or (to put it more exactly) the *homoousion* or so-called *homoiousion* should not be mentioned at all." These words are not scriptural, and the begetting of the Son is beyond understanding save to the Father and Son themselves. What is absolutely certain is the supremacy of the Father. "No one can doubt that the Father is greater in honor, dignity, splendor, majesty, and the name 'Father' itself." The Son himself testifies to the fact, when he says, "He who sent me is greater than I" (a contracted quotation of John 14:24, 28). The Illyrians go on to distinguish two *personae* of Father and Son. The Father is greater; the Son is "subject along with all the things that the Father has subjected to him." They differ also in attributes: The Father is without beginning, invisible, immortal, and impassible, whereas the Son, born "God from God, light from light" took "flesh or body, that is, man" and suffered through that humanity. The "conclusion and confirmation," in turn, of "the whole faith" is the need to preserve the Trinity. They quote the baptismal formula of Matt 28:19 and conclude by acknowledging the "Paraclete Spirit" who exists "through the Son" and was sent to "instruct, teach, and sanctify."

This statement is remarkable for its boldness. The Nicene *homoousion* was now becoming a rallying point for their opponents: Athanasius was defending it with vigor, and Western opponents of Valens and Ursacius had begun to advance the Nicene Creed at councils still under the Illyrians' effective control.[10] Though they laid claim to universal orthodoxy, Valens and Ursacius were really contributing to an unfolding controversy. To buttress their claim to orthodoxy, Valens and Ursacius wove in language familiar from the Eusebian tradition ("God from God, light from light," used at Antioch 341) and Tertullian (*personae, trinitas*). Equally familiar to Latin readers will have been the idea, shared by Tertullian, that the Son is visible in a way that the Father is not (chapter 1).[11] No less important, however, are the points at which they break with Tertullian. Hierarchical though his Trinity had been, Tertullian had readily accorded omnipotence to the Son.[12] He had also used the *substantia–persona* distinction to explain the relationships among the Father, Son, and Holy Spirit. Valens and Ursacius have rejected one of those paired terms as self-evidently unscriptural.

Where did this theology come from? The rejection of *ousia* terms would be repeated in the Homoian creed and paralleled by biblicist arguments from later Homoians (chapter 9). Were Valens and Ursacius simply trying to limit theology to the express words of scripture? Demonstrably not: The Bible never applies "person" (*persona*, Greek *prosōpon*) to the Father or Son in the Tertullianic, theological sense, yet Valens and Ursacius freely use the word. They are not staking out a distinctive theological method, but appealing to a universally agreed-upon norm—the authority of scripture—to head off any challenge to their claim that absolutely everyone agreed on the total supremacy of the Father.

Perhaps the best way, therefore, to explain how Valens and Ursacius got here is to say that the manifesto revealed a possibility that had been covered, all along, by the "big tent" of the Eusebian creeds. Those creeds attracted churchmen who held, like the late Eusebius of Caesarea, to a relatively high view of the Son, one that would lead to the Homoiousian formulations. The 341 creeds were also embraced by men—George of Laodicea once among them, ironically enough—who had been closely aligned with Arius and were willing to defend or reiterate his more extreme claims. Aëtius's teachers belonged to that camp, and Valens and Ursacius evidently stood somewhere near it, too. Orthodoxy, to their eyes, required a clear declaration of hierarchy within the Trinity: for now, granted the absence of controversy over the Holy Spirit, the absolute supremacy of the Father and the inferiority of the Son.[13] Those dogmas would, however, be best maintained without the philosophical language that could prove dangerous in the hands of the proponents of the Son's close likeness (let alone equality) to the Father.

## The Homoian Creed

### *Sirmium 359 and the Council of Rimini*

One term is conspicuous by its absence from the Sirmian manifesto: *homoios* itself. It entered at the Sirmian meeting of May 359. The "Dated Creed" proclaimed the Son to be "like the Father in all respects" and toned down the Homoians' initial objection to *ousia*.[14] As we saw in chapter 4, the creed satisfied neither Valens nor Basil of Ancyra. Later that year, Constantius II's grand ecumenical councils assembled: the Latins at Ariminum (Rimini) in Italy and the Greeks at Seleucia (Silifke) in Asia Minor. We will briefly describe the Eastern council in chapter 6. In the West, the Homoians met a strong pro-Nicene opposition. At the council's first session, the majority resolved to add nothing to the Nicene profession, endorsed *substantia* as a genuinely scriptural term, denounced numerous heresies including belief in "three divided substances" rather than "the one deity of the perfect Trinity" (a move that might have seemed dangerously modalist to the Homoians), and condemned Valens, Ursacius, and their allies.[15] Homoian defeat might have seemed certain, but Valens and Ursacius did not idly weather the council's denunciations. They met with their allies separately and, when the council sent ten delegates to await the emperor's return from the Persian frontier, a counter-slate of ten went as well.[16]

What happened next is obscure. The bare facts are known: As the weeks dragged on, the official delegates, who were staying at Nike in Thrace, retracted the council's condemnation.[17] They also endorsed a modified version of the "Dated Creed" that (among other altered points) forbade speaking of the Father, Son, and Holy Spirit as a single *hypostasis* (in Latin, presumably *substantia*) and declared the Son to be "like the Father . . . according to the scriptures," now without the phrase "in all respects" offensive to Valens.[18] On return to the council, the delegates alleged "force" by Constantius, but subtler maneuvering must have been involved, as well.[19] According to a Gallic council of the early 360s, the Homoian delegates had implied, deceitfully, that the Eastern bishops had already accepted the formula.[20] The Western bishops, still waiting at Rimini, slowly gave way. Our sources are pro-Nicene and hostile, but plausible. Valens won over the holdouts, not by clarifying his own doctrine, but by denouncing what really troubled them. To resounding agreement, he repeated the old condemnations of Arius's distinctive doctrines, including the claim that the Son was "a creature like other creatures."[21] Both Arius and Nicaea were excluded, and a new creedal baseline had been established—for a time.

## Early Homoian Theology
### *The Limits of Reconstruction*

What, then, was the theology that won out at Rimini? Did the world "groan"—in the famous words of Jerome—"and marvel that it was Arian"?[22] In literal terms, no. Even to say, however, that the Western bishops had accepted a "Homoian" consensus at Rimini is hardly sufficient. They seem to have endorsed a bland creed out of opposition to stereotyped "Arian heresy" and a desire to return to the ordinary business of their sees. To speak of the triumph of "Homoian doctrine" or the formation of a "Homoian consensus" would, in that context, be almost meaningless.

To search for Western Homoian doctrine in this early era is thus to ferret out the theological intentions of a kind of inner party. Actual data are few. The pro-Nicene Hilary of Poitiers says that he heard certain people—evidently, Greek Homoians inclined to Heteroousian theology—ask Valens and Ursacius why they had not declared the Son to be a created being. They answered that the bishops at Rimini had not denied it, only affirmed that the Son was unlike other created beings.[23] To pro-Nicenes, this was perfidy: Evidently, when Valens had affirmed at Rimini that the Son was not "a created being like other created beings," he had meant to hide a conviction that the Son was still a created being.[24] That inference is not nuanced enough. Hilary's report suggests that Valens did not, in fact, call the Son a created being in so many words. Such reticence would square well with the doctrine of later Western Homoians, who speak of the Son's having been "made" and "created," but never term him *creatura*, "a created being."[25] Still, it does place Valens and Ursacius closer to the Heteroousians than to the Homoiousians, let alone the pro-Nicenes.

What the anecdote does not do is establish that Valens's and Ursacius's thinking was representative of a united Homoian leadership—an inner party—at all. Serious differences of opinion soon came to divide them even from their Illyrian fellow signatory of the 357 manifesto. In December 366, Valens and Ursacius remonstrated with their old ally Germinius of Sirmium for affirming that the Son was "like the Father in all respects, except unbegottenness"—a view that threatened, they said, to restore the now-discredited doctrine of Basil of Ancyra.[26] In an open letter to their local Illyrian colleagues, Germinius appealed to a string of prooftexts to defend the likeness of Son to Father "in" (as he put it in a separate creedal statement) "divinity, charity, majesty, power, splendor, life, wisdom, and knowledge."[27] He was only defending the faith agreed at Sirmium in May 359, while his former allies wanted (so he alleged) to hold Christ to be like the Father in some respects, yet unlike in others.

To say that Germinius had ceased to be Homoian would be as incorrect as saying that Valens and Ursacius had actually joined the Heteroousians, who had by now separated into a church of their own (chapter 6).[28] None of the three Illyrians had repudiated Rimini or its creed. Germanius simply interpreted it through an expansive reading of its archetype, the "Dated Creed" of May 359, while Valens and Ursacius insisted that one should not go beyond what was actually affirmed at Rimini by veering toward Basil's Homoiousianism. That implies that they still held to the subordinationist convictions that had shaped the Sirmian manifesto of 357. We again encounter the problem of speaking of "Homoian" doctrine at Rimini, writ small.

A vague creed, devised through unwilling compromise with a party that had since been excluded from the winning alliance—a creed that had been adopted without clear agreement on its meaning—could, in time, become a symbol, by synecdoche, for a whole body of definite doctrines. But the set of people who held to it is likely to have been irreducibly diverse; and that, in the example of Germinius of Sirmium, is exactly what we find.

## Conclusion

Only over time could the Homoian creed come to mean something in particular, and only in contradistinction to other options. By opposing an interpretation of the creed that approached Homoiousianism, Valens and Ursacius took a distinguishing step. Pro-Nicene critics of those they termed "Arians" took many more. They did not necessarily succeed in their church-political aims. Ardent pro-Nicenes tried, and failed, to catch out Auxentius, whose appointment to the see of Milan had been engineered, in 355, by Valens and Ursacius.[29] Hilary reported his own failed effort in a furious tract *Against Auxentius*. To the satisfaction of the Western emperor, Valentinian I, Auxentius declared that he knew nothing of Arius or his teaching, endorsed the Rimini council, and issued a personal creed that called Christ "God the true Son from the true God, the Father."[30] To the vigilant Hilary, this seemed an implicit declaration that Christ was not "true God."[31] To others, Hilary may have seemed merely hypervigilant: and not without reason, granted that Germinius, for example, had spoken in similar terms.[32] In the long run, it did not matter. Auxentius died, still in his see, and was replaced by Ambrose, who would prove himself a pro-Nicene champion of exceptional skill.[33] Efforts such as Hilary's had not altered control over the Milanese church. They did hammer home the conviction that adherence to Rimini was a mark of heresy, and so help to shift the "Overton window" of acceptable theology away from it. Adherence to the Rimini creed, once general and so unremarkable, became a distinctive of those who held to the sharply subordinationist, anti-Nicene doctrine that we will begin to explore, through the teaching of the Gothic bishop Wulfila, in chapter 8.

We can see best where the Homoian core stood, once they are alone. In 381, Ambrose entrapped two Illyrian bishops, Palladius of Ratiaria (in northwest Bulgaria), an addressee of Germinius's self-defense, and Ursacius's successor Secundianus of Singidunum, at a small council held at Aquileia in northern Italy.[34] Ambrose tries to induce Palladius to condemn Arius's letter to Alexander (chapter 2). Remarkably, Palladius refused. His initial objections were procedural, and correct. Ambrose lacked authority, Palladius had not himself known Arius, and so on. Eventually, he gave in and began to argue doctrine. Under continuous pressure, Palladius failed to condemn not just Arius, but any of Arius's doctrines.[35] Palladius wrote an attack, shortly thereafter, on Ambrose's actions at the council. He incorporated part of an earlier counterblast to the first two books of Ambrose's *On the Faith*.[36] Here, he had answered Ambrose's claim that the "Arians" held the Son to be dissimilar to the Father with a rhetorical question: "if we confess what the Son has said, *For whatever the Father does, this also the Son does likewise* [John 5:19], how do we call him 'dissimilar'?"[37] The interpretation of the Homoian creed is exactly the one that George of Laodicea had anticipated, back when the creed was first formulated in May 359.[38] To deny that the Son was like the Father in essence was to affirm him alike only in will and activity. To hold to the Homoian creed was now, and would remain (chapters 8–9), to hold the Son a distinctly inferior, created being, the second stage in a sharply graded hierarchy below the Father, who alone is truly God.

CHAPTER 6

# Heteroousians

## *The "True Church" of Aëtius and Eunomius*

In the East, the Council at Seleucia unfolded in a way parallel, in one key parameter, to the Western Council of Rimini: The creed favored by the assembled bishops was not the Homoian creed eventually adopted. The Homoiousians mobilized the attendees around the Dedication Creed of Antioch 341.[1] A minority, including Aëtius's supporter Eudoxius of Antioch, met separately, under the leadership of Acacius, Eusebius's successor at Caesarea. This set of bishops enjoyed the support of the imperial officials overseeing the council. Two opposing slates of delegates went to Constantinople, met there with the delegates from Rimini, and, under pressure from Constantius, signed on to the Homoian creed on December 31, 359. The Eastern churches, too, now stood in formal agreement with the emperor's preferred creed.

Two vital church-political developments gave finer theological texture to the new Homoian alignment in the East. In its origin, the Homoian creed had been a compromise between the Illyrians and the Homoiousians. The Illyrians' 357 manifesto, however, had been welcomed in the East by churchmen—above all, Eudoxius—who were amenable to Aëtius. In 359/360, the Eastern Homoians broke with both alternatives. Seeking to win over naysayers at Seleucia, Acacius had already added a denunciation of "unlike" (*anomoios*) to his party's milder rejection of *homoousios* and *homoiousios*.[2] During the meeting in December 359, Aëtius angered Constantius II and was expelled.[3] His condemnation then became a key plank of the synod, firmly dominated by Acacius and Eudoxius, that met at Constantinople in 360.[4] The Homoian leadership also forced out key Homoiousians, largely on disciplinary grounds, and Eudoxius was appointed to the bishopric of Constantinople.[5]

In hindsight, these maneuvers did not reveal a united Homoian hierarchy in the East. Key leaders, including Eudoxius, sympathized with Aëtius's theology. Some, such as Eudoxius's allies Maris of Chalcedon and Euzoius of Antioch, even did so in a demonstrable commitment to the hard subordinationist tradition dating back to Arius's own day. They were aligned, however, with churchmen less willing to break with the Eusebian consensus of the 340s. Even Acacius, who had opposed the Homoiousian champions of the Dedication Creed at Seleucia 359, was not consistently radical. A firm anti-Marcellan, he was previously on record supporting "like in all things," and is said later, during a period of imperial favor for Nicaea, to have accepted the *homoousion*.[6]

To speak, therefore, of a single Homoian theology in the East in the 360s and 370s would make little more sense than for the West. We can mark out ideas held by certain adherents of the Homoian creed, but the history of Eastern Homoian Christianity during its ascendancy is mostly political and social: an account of bishops' actions and of the martyrs produced by local altercations during the brief reign of Julian (361–63), Constantine's pagan nephew.[7] Furthermore, works by later Greek-speaking churchmen with identifiably Homoian allegiance are almost completely lacking.[8] Some details reveal theological and churchly realignments, which we will discuss in chapter 10, but very little can be said about later Greek theology from the Homoian camp.

What we have, instead, are three theological alignments emerging from Constantius's councils that separate themselves ever more sharply from the imperial Homoian consensus. The first are the pro-Nicenes, now more open to the concept of multiple *hypostases* as explained by the Homoiousians in 358–359. The second are the so-called "Macedonians," Homoiousians who embraced a Nicene view of the Son, yet continued to hold the Holy Spirit at a level somewhere below full deity. The third is the only alignment to form a separate church of its own before the 380s: the Heteroousians who remained loyal to Aëtius and continued under the leadership of his stalwart and articulate disciple, Eunomius of Cyzicus. Though they agreed on many points with key signatories of the Homoian creed, these churchmen openly split with them, embracing the theological and disciplinary implications of Aëtius's thinking in all its radical fulness. Alongside the Macedonians (chapter 7), they were prime theological foils for the renewed pro-Nicene position elaborated by the Cappadocian Fathers Basil of Caesarea, Gregory of Nazianzus, and Gregory of Nyssa. They also present a case study in the formation of a self-consciously separatist church: one that can, in all fairness, be called, after a leader its adherents were eager to claim, "the Eunomians."

## Precision Theology

### *Aëtius and Eunomians Amid the Non-Nicene Trajectory*

Viewed from a distance, the Heteroousianism of Aëtius and Eunomius presents a subtle variation on the same broad theological pattern evidenced by the later Homoians (chapter 9) and indeed by the whole theological trajectory centered on likeness of will and the supremacy of the Unbegotten God back to Arius and Eusebius of Nicomedia (chapter 3). Viewed up close, however, it presents strikingly original features, which divide it from that theological trajectory on grounds quite oblique to Nicene preoccupation with issues of creation and divine equality.

The basic parameters were outlined by Aëtius, whose *Syntagmation* (chapter 4) provides the adept with succinct rebuttals against opponents he names "temporists." These are probably not members of the other well-known parties, but fellow Heteroousians at odds with Aëtius.[9] The hint of internal infighting is indicative. Despite Eunomius's attempts, in the immediate aftermath of Constantinople 360, to work with the dominant Homoian leadership, he and his followers would seek ever-greater accuracy of theological expression, without setting aside truth (as they saw it) for churchly harmony. Aëtius's extant theses are only a partial expression, however, of a theological system. For that, we must turn to the works of Eunomius. These include an *Apologia* delivered at Constantinople in 360, to the approval of the Homoians present;

another profession appended to it in the manuscript transmission; the fragments of a "second" apology, the *Apologia apologiae*, which defended his doctrines against a counterblast by Basil of Caesarea; and a brief *Exposition of the Faith* delivered, in more circumspect terms, at a council of the competing "sects" gathered by Theodosius I in 383 (chapter 7).[10] Across these works, Eunomius offered what appears to be a straightforward development of his teacher's project, with one notable exception. Where Aëtius identified deity directly with unbegottenness, Eunomius made it clear that the Son was, in fact, "begotten god" (a point particularly salient in the *Exposition of the Faith*).

To their opponents, including a Homoian such as Acacius of Caesarea, the Heteroousians were simply "Anomoians," believers that the Son was totally unlike (*anomoios*) the Father. That is caricature. The basis of their position did not lie in an imputation of simple unlikeness, but in two fundamental commitments. The first, illustrated by the staccato succession of Aëtius's syllogisms, was an uncompromising devotion to *precision* of theological method and expression. The second was the belief, which Aëtius's logic had upheld, that "unbegotten" is no mere predicate of God. The supreme being is precisely and indeed *completely* described by the term "unbegotten." These convictions were not just a matter of theological method and content; they also penetrated, as we will discuss later in the chapter, into their churchly practice, reworking sacramental rituals in ways now unfortunately obscure.

First, precision (*akribeia*, in Greek). In Heteroousian thought, devotion to tradition was displaced by a concern for successive experts who could uphold the flawless witness to divine exactitude preserved in the text of scripture.[11] The creeds of past councils—or even of illustrious teachers—play a minimal role in their arguments. At the outset of his *Apologia*, Eunomius does purport to be expounding the "precise" expression of the faith handed down "from the Fathers." The creed he quotes is, however, a stripped-down profession that merely outlines the names and most basic operations of the three Trinitarian persons.[12] Whether it is a genuinely traditional formulation or Eunomius's own distillation of Christian principles,[13] it is not the rallying creed of a churchly party.

He does not buttress his argument with proof of past consensus, but argues, in closer connection with the scriptural text than Aëtius in the *Syntagmation*, for the primacy of unbegottenness in discerning who and what God is.

This, the identification of the true God as the unbegotten according to essence, is the system's central doctrinal feature. Here, in fact, *unlikeness* does come in. As Aëtius had already outlined, "the same *ousia*" cannot be "both begotten and unbegotten." The Only-Begotten has to be a creation of God's power, not a separation from his own essence.[14] Offspring will remain offspring, and God will remain unbegotten: a fact that establishes the "incomparability in essence."[15] Following Aëtius, Eunomius held that God is truly one, simple, and not subject to deprivation: the essence of God is coincident with being the Unbegotten.[16] Unsurprisingly, he rejects equality of Father and Son as an absurd impiety.[17] He also draws another remarkable inference: The name "Father" does not indicate the essence of God. It is a mere designation for the ingenerate God, with respect to the action of begetting. To be Father was, therefore, an act of the will of the unbegotten God, and it is the Father's activity (his *energeia*) and his willing, identical with that activity, in which the Son is like him.[18] For Eunomius, to use the name "Unbegotten" is to give God "what he is owed: the agreement that he is what he is."[19]

That is an unmistakable allusion to the divine name revealed to Moses out of the burning bush (Exod 3). What has seemed to many Christians, however, to be the proclamation of ineffable *mystery* was to the Eunomians a full disclosure of *reality*. Under their reasoning lies a conviction that puts them at odds with their contemporaries. As Aëtius maintained, Christian hope stands or falls with the reality of the distinction between the unbegotten God and the begotten Son. He did not mean merely that "unbegotten" and "begotten" have to be valid *descriptors* of God and the Only-Begotten, but that, for Christianity to be valid, "unbegotten" and "begotten" must declare what the essences really *are*.[20] Thus, the church historian Socrates can quote a saying, attributed to Eunomius, that we know as much about God's essence as God does, while Socrates's Eunomian contemporary, Philostorgius, sees the doctrine of God's knowability as the fundamental dividing line between his own church and the Homoians.[21]

This doctrine marks an extraordinary break with the tradition of early fourth-century pro-Arian thinking. Arius had denied the knowability of God in the most extreme terms in his *Thalia*, and Eusebius of Nicomedia—though seen by Philostorgius as a champion of his own conviction (chapter 10)—had not disagreed.[22] The Eunomian rupture with this tradition, vitally, does not occur over any feature of the "Arian" or "Eusebian" tradition to which pro-Nicenes were regularly attuned: the Son's ontological subordination, his likeness to the Father in will and activity, or his "otherness" in essence. On those points, Eusebius of Nicomedia, the Eunomians, and indeed many signatories of the Homoian creed would have agreed heartily. Despite this agreement about the attributes of God, Aëtius and Eunomius were advancing a fundamentally different sensibility about the degree to which God is known: a sensibility that both rested upon and validated the claim to absolute precision in theology.

In Eunomian hindsight (again, Philostorgius's), that sensibility could seem the only reliable way to safeguard the doctrine of the ontological hierarchy of God, the Only-Begotten, and the Holy Spirit. The Son is fundamentally a creation of God, in spite (or because of) the Heteroousians' insistence on the language of offspring. If the essence of God is unbegotten/ingenerate (*age(n)nētos*), then it is truly said that the Son is Only-Begotten (*monogenēs*). To be made by the act of the Father's will, to be an "offspring," a "generate" or "begotten" thing (*gennēma*), accurately describes the essence of the Only-Begotten.[23] God's "relationship to the Son" (or perhaps, "the title Son") is a "bare appellation": They are just not the same sort of being at all.[24] Likewise, the firstborn of creation is, for Eunomius, of the same essence as creation.[25] As the confession appended to Eunomius's *Apologia* has it, the Son is a created being unlike any other created being, a thing made but not like any other thing made.[26] The underlying Aëtian conviction holds good even in Eunomius's *Exposition* of 383, which says that the Son is begotten

God, maker of all things, and perfect image of the Father. This imaging still takes place according to the will of God—the Son is the "seal of all the activity and power of the Almighty," receiving all things from his Father.[27] When that idea is coupled with the doctrine of God's knowability, we have a remarkable reconfiguration of the Christian awareness, raised so memorably by Arius in the *Thalia*, that human knowledge of God comes through Christ: for Eunomius, the incarnate Son really is the door, and to come to know the Son is to come to know God.[28]

Finally, the Holy Spirit is figured by Eunomius as a work of the Son, made at the command of the Father.[29] The Spirit is the only creation of its kind, and plays a crucial role in human salvation: It brings people into the mysteries, divides the gifts, and sanctifies through the will of the Son, which images the will of the Father.[30] This doctrine should not be conflated with an acceptance of a kind of mysticism, however, which was largely incompatible with the rationalism and precision favored by Eunomius and his fellow travelers. The Spirit is a creature of the Son who works his will in the world, strictly as described in scripture. The Spirit is third in order, below the Son, surpassing other creatures of the Son by being the first and best work of the Son as the Son is the first and greatest work of the Father.

## The Schismatic Drive

The basic results of Eunomian thought, as we have just sketched them, would have been welcome to anyone who stood consciously in the tradition of the early pro-Arian theologians, such as Eusebius of Nicomedia. It is little wonder, then, that the Heteroousians found support from surviving early Arians, including Maris of Chalcedon, a defender of Arius in 325, and Euzoius, Arius's fellow exile after Nicaea.[31] The underlying drive to precision, and the shocking implications about God's knowability that it entailed, were more of a problem. In the early 360s, Aëtius tried, it seems, to compromise, signing a creed that soft-pedaled divine knowability, perhaps to appeal to Eudoxius.[32] Eunomius, for his part, would work for some years with Eudoxius and Euzoius, aiming always for Aëtius's restoration, but was unwilling to sign off on the Homoian creed and its affirmation of the unknowability of the Son's begetting.[33]

The two Heteroousian leaders were unable, however, to reach an open alliance with either of these influential Homoian sympathizers. The reason was, in part, a matter of brute politics: Aëtius and Eunomius repeatedly linked themselves to members of the Constantinian dynasty who came to bad ends, including Constantius's tyrannical cousin Gallus (executed 354), Gallus's pagan half brother Julian (361–63), and the failed usurper Procopius (d. 366). The caution of cannier men does not surprise. At the most fundamental level, however, a theology built on absolute *precision* was not calibrated for compromise,[34] and the church-political hegemony of the Homoians rested upon a creed so broad it hardly had anything to compromise. Aëtius and Eunomius (and, often enough, Eudoxius himself) had no qualms about writing *pour épater les bourgeois*.[35] That was not going to yield consensus, in an Eastern church in which the majority of bishops had wanted, back in 359, simply to stick with the tried-and-true formula of Antioch 341. Over time, cagey churchmen might have pulled the consensus of Eastern bishops closer to their own position. But in the decisive early years of the 360s, to side with Aëtius and Eunomius might well, for Eudoxius and Euzoius, have meant breaking with the majority they had labored to build, in favor of a rigorist and offensive minority.

Separation from the mainstream church only came about through failed negotiations and miscommunications over the course of several years (chapter 10). Still, it was an all-but inevitable consequence of the radical expression of Heteroousian theology. Their convictions did not simply lie far from the mainstream—that might have been true of Eudoxius's or Euzoius's convictions, too. They were formulated in terms that confronted others with their radicalism. They also brought with them practical consequences, in the reshaping of the most basic Christian rituals, that would have set any churchman on guard. While pro-Nicene accounts vary from plausible to wild, it is certain that the Eunomians, at least at Constantinople, altered received baptismal practice, in ways that may have disturbed even some of their fellow

Heteroousians.[36] Baptism was performed "into the death of Christ": into the death, that is, of the begotten God in whose image the baptized could now share. Whether or not this was done upside down, as the more lurid accounts relate, it was done with a single immersion. This is the most profound ritual innovation that can be securely credited to any of the groups arising during the Arian controversy, and a fitting expression of the desire to achieve precision above all else.[37] Baptism, after all, really is into the Lord's death (Rom 6:3), and he died once.[38]

## Conclusion

In the 370s, the pro-Nicene Epiphanius penned a lurid portrait of Aëtius and his followers. Alleging their total disregard for the scriptural and customary limits upon Christian behavior (holiness of living, fasts, commandments), he accused them of reducing the requirements of the Christian faith down to the mere knowledge of God.[39] That claim has a strong resonance with Gregory of Nazianzus's jibe that the Eunomians made theologians of their believers in a single day.[40] Claims that they tolerated sexual immorality may be so much tittle-tattle, but this allegation rings more nearly true. Though the Eunomians did continue to make moral demands of other Christians,[41] and surely also of their own adherents, they reconfigured the common heritage of early Eusebian theology—and the common, baptismal heritage of all Christians—around the demand for absolute precision in the articulation of who and what God is. Here, though not in their basic convictions about God's unbegottenness, the secondary status of the Son, or the created non-deity of the Holy Spirit, the Eunomians differed decisively from the Homoians, whose own works reveal no major revisions to churchly practice (chapter 9).[42] The results remind one less of any other outcome of the wider Arian controversy than of the revisions to practice and theological articulation, driven by the *ressourcement* of scripture, on all sides of the sixteenth-century Reformation. In this regard, perhaps, the Eunomianism that petered out in the fifth century marked a road not taken.

# Part III

# Decline and Fall of the Homoians

CHAPTER 7

# The Turn to Pneumatology

WITH THE HARDENING of theological lines, a new battleground emerged: the status of the Holy Spirit. In fifth-century hindsight, this turn in the 350s, intensifying through the 360s and 370s, saw the formation of a new, "Macedonian" party, which denied the Spirit's deity.[1] The process culminated at the Council of Constantinople in 381, which the Council of Chalcedon 451 would later hold to have resolved the status of the Holy Spirit in line with the Nicene conclusion about the Son: The Holy Spirit is God, of one essence with the Father and the Son.

Though broadly correct, this traditional account has two major limitations. First, the terms are too clear-cut. While fifth-century church historians put the formation of a "Macedonian" alignment in the early 360s, there is no textual evidence to support the use of the term "Macedonian" prior to the 380s.[2] Application to the earlier period is a retrojection. Second, the so-called Pneumatomachi ("Spirit-fighters")—both Macedonians and distinct theological configurations that likewise denied the Holy Spirit's divinity—were not entirely innovative. Low pneumatologies had already been advanced in the third century.[3] What we are seeing is in fact a sharpening of distinctions, only embryonic in the 330s and 340s, in ways that partially crossed the pro-/non-Nicene lines. The relatively benign formulation of Antioch 341, retained by the Homoians in 357, had implied that the Holy Spirit was subordinate to the Son, but did not necessarily identify the Spirit as a created being. By the late 350s, some Egyptian churchmen of now-murky allegiance denied the ontological inferiority of the Son but asserted the Spirit's inferiority. In the 360s, low pneumatologies developed in two key directions. First, Eunomius's *Apologia* advanced a strong account of the tertiary status of the Spirit: As the Son's first and greatest creation, the Holy Spirit lacked the creative power distinctive of divinity. Second, after the Council of Lampsacus in 364, leading Homoiousians held the Spirit's deity in doubt, in terms that were notionally compatible with Nicaea 325. A partial convergence between the Homoiousian branch of Eusebian thought and a strictly coequalist reading of Nicaea, Macedonian pneumatology would prove a viable rival down to 383 and the formation of a lasting pro-Nicene consensus in the main, imperially sponsored church.

## Emerging Arguments

Eusebius of Caesarea's response, in 338, to Marcellus of Ancyra's discussion of John 15:26 is a typical expression of a mid-fourth-century low pneumatology.[4] Most of what Eusebius writes is directed at proving that the Holy Spirit is distinct from the Father and the Son, since Eusebius reads as Sabellian Marcellus's argument that the Father, Son, and Spirit belong to the "oneness" of God (chapter 3). As Eusebius concludes his arguments, he describes the Spirit as a part of the Trinity and greater than any created being.[5] The Spirit is, however, subordinate to the Son (so John 16:13–14). Eusebius notes that the angels are also spirits (Heb 1:7), but places the Holy Spirit above them. All things, including the Holy Spirit, are made through the Son.[6]

Eusebius stops short of describing the Holy Spirit as an angel or as a creature, but he has set the (independent) ontological status of the Son and Spirit at a lower level than that of the Father, in opposition to Marcellus's apparently modalist view, already condemned at Tyre 335. Given the relative reserve on the subordination of the Spirit in the creed of Antioch 341, Eusebius's words represent the earliest articulation of what can be termed an "anti-Nicene" pneumatology only in a loose sense. It clashed with the positions taken by Nicaea's early defenders, such as Marcellus and Athanasius, and with the later pro-Nicene consensus, but in fact was perfectly coherent with the extremely limited pneumatological article ("and in the Holy Spirit") of Nicaea 325.

The next development in almost-anti-Nicene pneumatology emerges in 358, when Athanasius's letters to Serapion of Thmuis describe a group called *Tropikoi* ("trope-mongerers"). Though probably limited to Egypt, they advanced arguments parallel both to Eusebius's earlier and to Eunomius's later positions.[7] Per Athanasius's report, the Tropikoi were former Arians, who had recanted their belief in the Son's inferiority but resisted the claim that the Spirit was likewise God.[8]In their eyes, the Holy Spirit is not God, but rather a created being, distinct from other angels in degree rather than kind.[9] Their belief that the Spirit is a created being appears to turn largely on Amos 4:13, in which God declares that he creates spirits. This is a crucial passage for the debates over the Spirit, appearing in nearly all Nicene counterarguments. Less widely disputed, but apparently significant to the Tropikoi, is 1 Timothy 5:21.[10] The ordering in which Paul charges Timothy, in the sight of God, Jesus, and the angels, is taken to suggest that the Spirit must be counted among them. In his third letter, Athanasius repeats further questions apparently posed by this group. Appealing to John 16:14, they ask whether the Spirit, if he is not a created being and receives from the Son what is given by the Father, would be a grandson of the Father.[11]

In the third letter, Athanasius also refines his positioning of the Tropikoi among the "Arian" theologians. Their beliefs were similar, he writes, to those of opponents, including Eunomius, Eudoxius, Eusebius (presumably of Nicomedia), and Acacius of Caesarea.[12] This need not mean, of course, that the pneumatologies held by these disparate parties rested on the same theological and scriptural basis, but Athanasius would be proved broadly right. In time, both Homoians and Eunomians formulated views of the Holy Spirit parallel to that of the Tropikoi, yet without their acceptance of the Son's equality to the Father.

Advanced at the Council of Constantinople 360, Eunomius's first *Apologia* was intended to demonstrate the consistency of his beliefs with those of the Homoians, then led by Acacius. While the resultant conciliar creed—a lightly modified version of the creed of Rimini 359—only asserts a belief in the Spirit and his sending as the Comforter by Jesus,[13] it is reasonable to assume that the pneumatology of the *Apologia* was agreeable to contemporary Homoians: enough so that Eunomius was briefly appointed to the see of Cyzicus at Eudoxius's direction.

As we have already seen briefly in chapter 6, Eunomius's pneumatology displays all his characteristic crispness of logic. The Spirit is third in order, dignity, and consequently also in nature.[14] He is a "thing made" (*poiēma*), fashioned by the creative power of the Son at the command of the Father (an argument resting on passages such as John 1:3). The Spirit is the only creation of its kind, not possessing a share of divinity or the power of creation, but possessing the powers of instruction and sanctification.[15] The Spirit is the totally subordinate creature of the Son, who is in turn subordinate to and made by the Father. Eunomius makes no reference to the angels and sharpens the creaturely status of the Spirit, implied by theologians such as Eusebius, to its finest possible point: so sharp, in fact, that Basil of Caesarea could write, a few years later, that Eunomius was the first person he had ever heard refer to the Spirit in such terms.[16] Basil may well have been right about the position's novelty. Aëtius's *Syntagmation* contains no mention of the Holy Spirit. Certainly, none of the Homoiousian or Homoian creeds went so far: the Dedication Creed of Antioch 341, still retained by the Homoiousians, spoke vaguely of gradation in "honor," while the various forms of the Homoian creed from 359–360 only suggested the subordination of the Spirit in his sending by the Son—not a controversial stance.

In this context, Eunomius's forcefulness was perhaps ill-considered. Certainly, by 383 and the composition of his *Exposition* for the "council of the sects" at Constantinople (discussed further below), his language had become more moderate. There, the Spirit is "generated by the only God through the Only-Begotten and made subject to him." Gone were the arguments from order and the language of making that had been maligned in the interim by Basil and by Gregory of Nyssa.[17] A last attempt to assert his theology's orthodoxy in the face of imperial hostility, this profession failed, and Eunomian influence over church politics would continue to fade (chapter 10). Still, Eunomius's articulation of a Heteroousian pneumatology had an enduring impact on late fourth-century theology. The first comprehensive pro-Nicene treatment of the Holy Spirit, Didymus's *De Spiritu Sancto*, responded to him as well as to local, Alexandrian Pneumatomachi.[18] At the other theological extreme, the pneumatology of the later Homoians, first attested in 383, would closely resemble Eunomius's (chapter 8).

## The Macedonian Party

Around the same time that Eunomius was circulating his *Apologia*, a new alignment began to take shape around the Homoiousian Macedonius of Constantinople. Under the direction of Acacius and Eudoxius, Constantinople 360 not only deposed Eunomius's mentor Aëtius, but also deposed Macedonius—in favor of Eudoxius himself—and Eleusius of Cyzicus, who was replaced by Eunomius.[19] Socrates directly connects the emergence of a Macedonian party to the deposition of Macedonius. After his ejection from Constantinople, Macedonius drew together a party that affirmed the *homoiousios* and the Dedication Creed. Socrates goes on to relate that, at some later point, Macedonius denied the divinity of the Spirit. His ally Eustathius—likewise condemned or deposed at Constantinople 360—replied that he could call the Spirit neither God nor a created being. Thus, their party was called "Pneumatomachi."[20] The appellation "Macedonians" seems, therefore, to have referred initially to Macedonius's Homoiousian allies, without reference to pneumatology: possibly the reason why it only became a synonym for Pneumatomachi in the 380s.

Given that Macedonius is supposed to have died not long after his deposition, his association with his party's later pneumatological position may be fictitious. The most significant figures in the movement bearing Macedonius's name appear to be Eustathius of Sebaste and Eleusius of Cyzicus. A third essential figure was Marathonius, who embraced the monastic life at Eustathius's urging; by supporting the Macedonian movement monetarily, he prevented it from being eliminated entirely in Constantinople.[21] Both Macedonius and Marathonius are credited with the invention of the term *homoiousios*, and so with an important role in the formulation of Homoiousian thought.[22] Unsurprisingly, their low pneumatology went on to rupture the fragile rapprochement, begun in the late 350s, between supporters of *homoousios* and of *homoiousios*. In 364, the Macedonians reached a pivotal moment. Meeting at Lampsacus on the Hellespont, they affirmed the Dedication Creed and condemned Acacius and Eudoxius, as well as the creed of Rimini.[23] As the Homoians continued to press their opponents, a delegation including Eustathius and two others (Theophilus of Castabala and Silvanus of Tarsus) went to Liberius of Rome and expressly endorsed Nicaea.[24] They carried back a positive reply from Liberius.[25] It seems implausible that Liberius should have been unaware of the views on the Spirit prevailing among Eustathius and his "Macedonian" friends. Why, then, was he supportive?

An earlier East–West connection may help to explain the unexpected Western support for a low pneumatology: Hilary of Poitier's attempt at conciliation in 358 in *On the Councils*. Hilary writes approvingly of his "holy brothers," Basil of Ancyra, Eustathius, and Eleusius, imploring them to affirm the *homoousion* even if alongside the *homoiousion*.[26] In a pro-Nicene exegesis of the Dedication Creed, Hilary affirms that it was more appropriate to proclaim "a unity on the basis of harmony (*consonantia*, equivalent to the Greek *symphōnia*) than of essence through similarity of substance," since the Holy Spirit was mentioned.[27] At this point, the general position that the *homoousion* ought not be extended to the Holy Spirit appears to have been acceptable even to a Western pro-Nicene.[28] Likewise, the later pro-Nicene champion Basil of Caesarea, with whom Eustathius visited at Eusinoe before the council, can hardly have been unaware of his old friend's pneumatology.[29] Such affiliations doubtless contributed to the anxiety felt by Gregory of Nazianzus over Basil's pneumatology, as well as the scholarly suspicion, still sometimes found, that, among the three Cappadocians, Basil had the greatest reserve with respect to the Spirit's deity.[30]

In the early 360s, therefore, the pro-Nicene consensus on the Spirit's deity had not yet fully hardened. It is possible, therefore, that Lampsacus produced a commitment to Nicaea, just one that read its pneumatological article through the lens of the Dedication Creed. If the bishops' pneumatology was something like that which Socrates attributed to Eustathius—that he was unwilling either to call the Spirit God or to state, with Eunomius, that the Spirit was the Son's created work—then it is plausible that at least some pro-Nicenes still preferred the Macedonians to the Homoians. Later, however, the lines would be drawn with more clarity, and the Macedonians, like the Homoians and Eunomians, would be left out of the pro-Nicene imperial consensus of the 380s.

## Macedonian Pneumatology

All our substantive evidence for the pneumatology of the new party that had formed around Macedonius, Eleusius, and Eustathius comes from pro-Nicene works that condemned the party's teaching. Works written by all three Cappadocian Fathers indicate that the views of the Macedonians (as they would, by the 380s, definitely be termed) reflect the position credited to Eustathius. In a generous passage, Gregory of Nazianzus allows that doubters of the Spirit's divinity still to a degree "partake of him." He implies that those to whom he directed his comments did not go so far as to attribute servitude to the Spirit. On this basis, Gregory holds that they must then place the Spirit in the same rank as God.[31] He suggests that if they could show him a halfway point between lordship and servitude, he would himself place the Spirit there. That puts these opponents somewhere near Eustathius's view and far from Eunomius or the later Homoians, since Nazianzen condemns those who held the Spirit to be created as "the worst of the wicked."[32] Just whom he has in mind, he does not explicitly say, but it is probably the allies of Macedonius—an inference supported by Gregory of Nyssa, whose anti-Pneumatomachian treatise avers that there was no new thing in a borderland between created and uncreated, and says that his opponents separate the Spirit from "creative force."[33] That was a view less extreme than idea that the Spirit was of created nature, whose proponents, in Nyssen's view like Nazianzen's, were not to be counted as Christians at all. The Macedonians' use of 1 Timothy 5:21 likewise points to the relative ambiguity or moderation of their position. While the Tropikoi used the verse to suggest the Spirit was an angel, Basil implies that the Macedonians suggested that things other than those divine may be numbered with the Father and the Son without being the object of worship.[34] Macedonian pneumatology may thus be placed at the midpoint of the developed pro-Nicene and anti-Nicene (Homoian or Eunomian) positions: The Spirit is not a creator, but is not properly a created being. The Spirit possesses those powers necessary for the salvific actions the Spirit is described as taking, but no more.

## A Slow Separation
### *Constantinople 381–83*

The halfway pneumatology of the Macedonians was as unacceptable to the emerging pro-Nicene consensus as was the explicit identification of the Spirit as a creature, which became the defining pneumatological belief of the Homoians and the Eunomians alike. A common element is shared across the whole emerging tradition of (in time, distinctly) non-Nicene low pneumatology, including Eusebius of Caesarea, Eunomius, the later Homoians (chapter 8), Macedonianism as portrayed by the Cappadocians, and even the mildly subordinationist creeds from the 340s and 350s. This element is the conviction that the Spirit is not a creator.[35] Scriptural witness secured the gift giving and sanctifying role of the Spirit in all these accounts, but the absence or presence of this creative function operated as marker distinguishing the Homoian, Homoiousian, and Heteroousian accounts from the Nicene position promulgated explicitly at the Council of Constantinople in 381, which expanded the 325 Nicene Creed to say that the Spirit is the "Lord, the giver of Life."[36] On the traditional view, owed to the council of Chalcedon and the fifth-century pro-Nicene historians, this declaration marked a decisive rejection of Macedonian as well as Homoian and Eunomian Trinitarian theologies. Now backed by Theodosius I and paralleled by Ambrose's maneuverings at Aquileia (also in 381), the new pro-Nicene consensus of the Eastern church left no room for

Macedonian ambiguity on the status of the Spirit: Either the Spirit was a creator like the Father and the Son, or a creature.

In fact, the developments on the ground were slower and more complex than theological hindsight makes them.[37] Pro-Nicene works opposing Macedonian pneumatology were indeed joined by a legal pronouncement from Theodosius asserting that the "one deity" and "equal majesty" "of the Father, Son, and Holy Spirit" were to be believed. However, this first law, of February 380, had in fact preceded Constantinople 381, and was only one step in a shifting imperial outlook.[38] It made the teachings of Damasus of Rome and Peter II of Alexandria normative for the churches under Theodosius's sway. When the council met in May 381, all would not go nearly so smoothly as this Theodosian prospectus had suggested it should—for reasons as much to do with internal pro-Nicene schisms as with substantive theological disagreement.

One hundred and eighty-six Eastern bishops attended the council, which convened under Meletius, Acacius's appointee (in 360) to the see of Antioch. Though seen by many as a champion of Nicaea, Meletius was still in schism with Paulinus, leader of the city's original Nicene faction, which had formed in the 320s, upon the deposition of the city's eminent pro-Nicene bishop Eustathius (chapter 2).[39] Since Damasus supported Paulinus, Meletius's presidency put the council at odds with one of Theodosius's normative bishops.[40] That Meletius was presiding at all was owed, furthermore, to the failure of the Egyptian delegation, including Theodosius's other normative bishop, Peter of Alexandria, to arrive (unsurprisingly, granted that Peter had died three months prior). When Meletius himself died, he was replaced by Gregory of Nazianzus, without support from the now-present Egyptians. The question of Meletius's replacement came before the council. Gregory backed Paulinus, but saw support collapse, as the presbyter Flavian was ordained bishop instead.[41] From this weakened position Gregory began to lead the doctrinal work of the council and attempted to establish a consensus in favor of the Godhood and consubstantiality of the Spirit.

In the meantime, thirty-six "Macedonian" bishops had been turned away, doubtless through Gregory's influence, for their failure to assent to the Nicene Creed.[42] According to Gregory, the council sought a compromise position, presumably at Theodosius's urging.[43] Betrayed by Gregory of Nyssa and under increasing pressure over technical irregularities in his assumption of the Constantinopolitan bishopric, Gregory surrendered the conciliar presidency, gave up the see of Constantinople, and departed.[44] The council ended with a declaration by Theodosius, in July 381, of the "one majesty and power," "the same glory," and "unity of divinity" of the Father, Son, and Holy Spirit.[45] The "undivided substance" (i.e., *homoousion*) "of the Trinity," asserted in a law of January 381, was absent.[46] The July law lists nine Eastern bishops, including Timothy of Alexandria and Gregory of Nyssa. The architects of compromise were therefore elevated to the status of normative bishops, like the now-deceased Peter and the still-living Damasus in 380. Constantinople 381 therefore concluded with no reconciliation at Antioch, Gregory of Nazianzus out of power despite his strong support for the Spirit's equal deity, and the formulation of a creed that did not directly affirm the Spirit's share in the one divine *ousia* of the Father and the Son.[47] The Macedonian position, which associated the Spirit with the Father and Son without exactly making him God, was excluded on the grounds of worship and the creative role of the Spirit, but not on the unambiguous ground of a common essence.

This compromise did not last long. Damasus of Rome was greatly displeased by the ordination of a previously unbaptized civil official, Nectarius, to the see of Constantinople. Another synod met in 382.[48] In the meantime, Damasus very likely sent his own theological declaration (the *Tome of Damasus*) to the East, in which he absolutely excluded compromise positions on the Spirit's deity. Theodosius, who had not given up hope of resolving the church's ongoing divisions, or at least of seeing what groups could be included under Nicaea, instructed Nectarius to convoke a third synod of the disparate "sects" in 383.[49] Through the maneuverings of a small, separatist pro-Nicene church at Constantinople, the Novatianists, what was designed as a debate turned into a submission of set statements of faith for the emperor to review. The leaders are listed by Socrates (himself possibly Novatianist, and attuned to their traditions): Nectarius and the Novatianist Agelius for the *homoousion*, Demophilus for the (Homoian) Arians, Eunomius for the Eunomians, and Eleusius for the Macedonians. Only those statements containing the *homoousion* were accepted, while the others were rejected for "introducing division into the Trinity."[50] The result was an anti-Macedonian hardening of the position adopted only two years prior, as Theodosius issued punitive edicts against a host of sects, including Eunomians and Arians/Homoians, but also Pneumatomachians and Macedonians.[51]

In the West, Homoians continued to receive the favor of the young Valentinian II and his mother, Justina, which issued, in 385–86, in a famous contest between Ambrose and the imperial court at Milan over control of the local basilicas.[52] However, all non-Nicene theologies had received a severe blow, one that would be confirmed upon Theodosius's assumption, in 394, of control over the entire empire. From the 380s onward, to be a Christian—to be a member of the church as acknowledged by the emperor and governed by the main hierarchy of bishops—implied, and required, an adherence to the fully developed theology of Nicaea. Debate over the coequal deity of the Father, the Son, and the Holy Spirit would now take place across the boundaries of rival churches, not within the confines of one formally undivided church.

CHAPTER 8

# Gothic Homoianism

A FEW YEARS before the councils of Constantinople and Aquileia in 381, events had begun to unfold that would prove decisive for the future of non-Nicene Christianity and the Roman Empire itself. Beyond the empire's frontier on the River Danube, Germanic-speaking tribes had come under pressure from the nomadic Huns. In 376, a group of Goths crossed the Danube into Roman territory. Mistreated by local officials, they revolted. Meanwhile, an element of a second Gothic tribe crossed the Danube unopposed. The united Gothic forces met the emperor Valens and his army near Adrianople (Edirne, in European Turkey) on August 9, 378. The battle was a total victory for the Goths. Valens was killed, along with two-thirds of his field army. Over the ensuing decades, the Roman authorities would fail to assimilate these Goths and their descendants. After a breakdown in relations in the early 400s, they invaded Italy. In 410, they sacked Rome: the first foreign capture of the Eternal City in eight hundred years.[1]

Though politically secondary due to the absence of the Western emperor's court (now based at Ravenna), the sack of Rome was a major symbolic moment in the disintegration of the Western Roman Empire. As Roman rulership crumbled, new polities took shape. The non-Roman elites of the Visigoths (descendants of Valens's foes) in western France and Spain, the Vandals in North Africa, the Ostrogoths in Italy, and the Burgundians in eastern France accepted the Homoian creed of 359–360 and rejected the pro-Nicene consensus of the 380s.[2] Very little is known about the process by which these peoples embraced Homoian Christianity, but the foundation was in place by the 340s.[3] No later than the Council of Antioch of 341, a Gothic churchman was ordained by Eusebius of Nicomedia.[4] In Greek, his name was represented as *Oulphilas*;

in Latin, as *Ulfila*. The underlying Gothic is probably "Wulfila." He was a descendant of Christians taken captive by the Goths in the 250s. Driven, with other Christian Goths, from Gothic territory when persecution broke out in the late 340s, Wulfila settled on the Roman side of the Danube—the heartland of non-Nicene Christianity in the Latin-speaking world. He not only signed the Homoian creed at Constantinople 360.[5] He was also responsible for the translation of the Bible into Gothic and is said to have conducted vigorous theological activity in Gothic, Latin, and Greek alike.[6]

Wulfila was a peripheral player within the Eusebian and Homoian alliances. By a remarkable turn of historical fortunes, he set the trend for later non-Nicene Christianity nonetheless. From the 380s to the final rejection of "Arian" thought by the Visigoths in 589, non-Nicene theology was accepted chiefly among Germanic-speaking, barbarian peoples. In this chapter, we will describe non-Nicene "Gothic theology" in two senses. The first sense refers to the theology *of a non-Nicene Goth*—of the only Gothic-speaking churchman we know in any detail. What did Wulfila perceive as orthodoxy, and how did his teaching relate to contemporary non-Nicene thought as a whole? The second is the kind of teaching that was available to Homoians *in Gothic*. What theology do the remnants of Gothic literature embody? What would a non-Nicene, Gothic-speaking churchman have received as orthodoxy through the writings produced by Wulfila and others?

## The Theology of a Goth

### *Wulfila's Creed*

Due to his biblical translation, Wulfila was a key influence on Gothic-speaking Christianity as a whole. We will therefore begin at the end: with Wulfila's deathbed profession of faith. Here, we benefit from an extraordinary chance of textual preservation. Palladius of Ratiaria, Ambrose's main target at Aquileia 381, wrote a protest against the synod.[7] A portion is preserved on the margins of a fifth-century manuscript of anti-Arian works by Hilary and Ambrose.[8] Palladius's comments are prefaced by a rambling introduction from a bishop named Maximinus and are followed by a concluding section, written by the same Maximinus, that comments on laws from the 380s reproduced in the *Theodosian Code* of 438.[9] Maximinus shares his name with a Homoian bishop who came to North Africa in 427 and disputed with Augustine in a live debate, preserved as Augustine's *Conference with Maximinus* (*Conlatio cum Maximino*; chapter 9).[10] Very likely, they are the same man. As a testimony to the orthodoxy of Palladius and of Arius himself, Maximinus cites a letter, written shortly after Wulfila's death, by Auxentius, bishop of the Danubian border town of Durostorum (Silistra, Bulgaria), who was known to Palladius and may have been an opponent of Ambrose in the mid-380s.[11]

This letter promises a unique window onto the thinking of the man who, more than any other, ensured the survival of non-Nicene Christianity after its rejection by the Roman emperors. Many sides claimed Wulfila.[12] The fifth-century pro-Nicene church historians cast him as a late convert (in 360 or the 370s) to "Arian" heresy.[13] That is improbable. A man closely connected to Eusebius of Nicomedia will always have been an "Arian" in the loose sense used by pro-Nicenes. The Eunomian church historian Philostorgius claimed Wulfila for his own, Heteroousian doctrine: more plausibly, as we will see, but only so long as one overlooks actual church membership.[14] Auxentius alone is a contemporary, and Auxentius alone can claim personal knowledge of Wulfila.

The letter begins with a lengthy disquisition on Wulfila's teaching and ends with Wulfila's deathbed profession. Both are profoundly subordinationist. Auxentius opens with a grand set of titles for the "One Only True God, the Father of Christ": he is "Ingenerate" or "Unbegotten" (*ingenitum*), "without beginning, without end, everlasting, on-high, sublime, superior, the most high Author . . . invisible, immeasurable, immortal, incorruptible," and a whole chain of descriptors that, mostly by negation, express God's absolute transcendency over created being. This God, Auxentius says, "created and begat, made and established, the only-begotten God." Christ, Wulfila taught, was "second God and author of all things from the Father, after the Father, on account of the

Father, and to the glory of the Father." He, too, receives a list of titles: "Great God, Great Lord, Great King, Great Mystery . . . the lawgiver, the redeemer," and other appellations that overlap at no point, save "God" and "author," with the Father's.[15] Wulfila did not simply teach, therefore, that the Son was "similar to the Father . . . according to the divine scriptures and tradition" (an echo of the Homoian creed of 359–360). He asserted the "distinctness" of Father and Son, in opposition to the Homoousians, Homoiousians, and Macedonians alike. All assimilated the Son too closely to the Father and failed to recognize "that the Father is indeed creator of a creator, but the Son is creator of all creation; and the Father is God of the Lord, but the Son is God of all creation."[16]

The pattern familiar from the Sirmian manifesto of 357 (chapter 5) has hardened. It has also expanded to encompass the Holy Spirit. In 357, Valens and Ursacius had retained the pneumatology of Antioch 341. Doubtless, they believed that the Spirit belonged in third rank, as the Dedication Creed had declared, but they did not emphasize his subordination. Auxentius, by contrast, declares that the Holy Spirit was "made by the Father through the Son before all things" and belongs "in third place."[17] Wulfila's creed sets up a yet-steeper hierarchy.[18] The Father is "God of all, who is also God of Our God," but the Holy Spirit is "the illuminating and sanctifying Power . . . neither God nor our God, but a minister of Christ . . . subject and obedient in all things to the Son; and the Son subject and obedient also in all things to his God and Father."[19]

In a preamble, Wulfila claims to have always believed the doctrines he expounds. That claim was doubtless sincere, but it likely reflects an old man's hindsight. The Holy Spirit takes up about as much space in Wulfila's creed as do the Father and the Son combined. Wulfila can hardly have been expounding the doctrine of which he had been conscious since the 340s, when he will have accepted one of the creeds of Antioch, or 360, when he embraced the Homoian creed. In response to the catastrophe (as Homoians will have seen it) of 381, he was drawing out the view of the Holy Spirit that seemed, in hindsight, always to have been implicit in the teaching he had accepted throughout his life.

This new and harder subordinationism is universally accepted by the non-Nicene Latin texts that survive from the 380s and after (chapter 9). Wulfila and Auxentius represent the new mainstream of a narrowed Homoian movement, which was, for the first time, becoming a well-defined church of its own. To some modern scholars, the strength of Wulfila's subordinationism has seemed to make him and the other late Homoians appear more Eunomian than Homoian.[20] That is an error, but an error that grasps an important truth, one to which we already gestured in chapter 5. Auxentius pits Wulfila against many rival groups.[21] The Eunomians are not among them, and in fact their doctrine of God never comes in for criticism in surviving Homoian texts written after 381.[22] This does not mean that the two churches coalesced or that Wulfila's views were fully compatible with Eunomian convictions, especially about God's knowability or the need to use rigorous *ousia* language.[23] To call the later Homoians "Homoians" is, however, to refer only, through convenient shorthand, to the creed advanced at Rimini–Seleucia, Nike, and Constantinople 360. Its adherents were "Riminists," in the sharp sense that they rejected Nicaea and the *homoousion*.[24] Their doctrinal differences with the Eunomians were objectively slight (chapter 10), incorporating a strong gradation from an absolutely divine Father, through a divine Son who was a "created creator," to a mighty but nondivine Holy Spirit. That gradation was first clearly articulated, among all our extant Homoian authors, by the dying Wulfila.

## Theology in Gothic

### *The Skeireins and the Gothic Bible*

If Wulfila's creed was a product of hindsight, what kind of theology passed into Gothic before the 380s? Any answer must be tentative and incomplete, since the Gothic language survives in fragments. Though a dialect was still spoken in the Crimea in the sixteenth century, all varieties of Gothic are now extinct. The vast bulk of the extant material consists of biblical manuscripts, all produced in Ostrogothic Italy.[25]

We have large chunks of the gospels and the Pauline epistles. From the Old Testament, a portion of Nehemiah survives. Otherwise, the only significant texts are several entries in a liturgical calendar for October and November, part of a sermon or lengthy prayer (the "Bologna fragments"), and eight pages of a commentary on John, now dubbed the *Skeireins* ("interpretation").[26]

What is most remarkable about the Gothic texts, as an ensemble, is in fact how nonpartisan they are. The liturgical calendar is clearly non-Nicene, with feasts in memory of the pro-Homoian emperor Constantius II and Dorotheus, the Homoian bishop of Constantinople (d. 407). Pro-Nicenes, however, could praise even "Arianizing" Gothic martyrs,[27] and the other figures commemorated by the liturgical calendar are the completely uncontroversial apostles. A vital testimony to Gothic churchly practice, the calendar most likely originated at Constantinople sometime after 419, where a Gothic community, consisting largely of soldiers in imperial service and their families, had continued under Wulfila's former secretary, Selenas.[28] The Bologna fragments, on the other hand, contain no overtly Homoian elements at all.[29]

The same is true of the biblical text translated, or at least curated, by Wulfila. Scholars have long sought traces of "Arianism" in the remnants of the Gothic text. That quest has failed. The Gothic New Testament is a reasonably competent rendering of a Greek original that is rather different from the texts reconstructed by modern New Testament scholars.[30] It contains some errors, but also some points of clever translation. Variations in the rendering of certain words—in particular, *arkhiereus* ("high priest") in John—suggest the involvement of multiple translators.[31] The Gothic can accentuate the theological impact of a key pro-Nicene prooftext (John 10:30, rendered with a rare dual verb form, rather than a plural: "I and my father are-(both) one"). While we can never be sure how such passages sounded to native Gothic speakers, the Gothic Bible displays nothing like the systematic subordinationism of the most notable modern anti-Trinitarian version, the *New World Translation* used by the Watch Tower Bible and Tract Society (Jehovah's Witnesses).

The key exception has always seemed to be the rendering of Philippians 2:6. Here, the Gothic translates "[Christ] did not think it robbery to be equal with God" as "[Christ] did not think it robbery to be alike to God." Naively, one might suppose this to be a (literally) Homoian mistranslation, and yet it is out of step with the interpretation seemingly preferred by later Homoians such as Maximinus (that Christ, who was not equal to God, did not presume to "rob" such equality for himself).[32] The Gothic translator—presumptively, Wulfila—has remodeled the following verses, too, breaking the parallel between "the form of God" and "the form of a servant," and replacing it with a new parallel between being "alike to God" and taking on "the likeness of men." He appears, in fact, to be presenting what modern biblical scholars call a "functionally equivalent" or "dynamic" translation. He is altering the literal wording in order to draw out the meaning discerned within it by a long line of Greek exegetes, including Origen, Eusebius of Caesarea, and the Homoiousians of the 350s, but not by more stringent "Arians."[33] The motivation might have had something to do with the Gothic implications of talk about a "form" of God. At any rate, it means that the most theologically laden translational choice within the extant portions of the Gothic New Testament does not present the hard subordinationist doctrine later embraced by Wulfila, but an earlier theological position with a higher view of the Son.[34]

Something similar is true of the *Skeireins*. Eight pages allow only the barest glimpse of the work's doctrines, but the remnants are enough to reveal its origin. Direct verbal overlap with two fragments preserved in Byzantine Greek anthologies shows that the *Skeireins* is a translation of the now-lost John commentary by Theodore of Heraclea, a member of the commission that investigated Athanasius in 335 and a fixture at Eusebian councils down to 351.[35] What remains is largely uncontroversial. The commentator discourses on baptism, Christ's work as a divine teacher, the superiority of his teaching to the Jewish law, and the place of John the Baptist as a divinely ordained forerunner to Christ. He also implies that Christ was a divine spirit directly indwelling a human body.[36] After the 360s, pro-Nicenes generally held that the Son had taken on both a human soul and a human body. In the 340s and 350s, however, this Christology was routine enough that Athanasius could regularly speak of the assumption of "flesh" by the divine Word without discussing Christ's human soul.[37] One other point would have attracted more controversy: Leaf V of the *Skeireins* asserts that "like," but not "equal," honor is owed to the Son as to the Father. That wording would have resonated with later Homoians, but the subordinationism of the extant leaves is otherwise muted. The target is not yet Homoousian doctrine as such, but Marcellus of Ancyra and his allegedly modalist views.[38] Like Gothic Philippians, the *Skeireins* therefore preserves a layer of early, Eusebian thought that Wulfila himself had abandoned by the end of his life.

## Conclusion

Late antique Christians were not blind to the ethnic differences that divided Romans from Goths and other Germanic speakers. Ambrose of Milan tried to discredit the Homoian churchman Julianus Valens for adopting Gothic customs.[39] In the 440s, the monk Salvian of Marseille, a harsh critic of his own Roman people, credited the barbarians' acceptance of "heresy" to corrupted copies of the Bible (quite wrongly, as we have seen).[40] But ancient writers rarely raise enmity for barbarians as a reason to oppose Homoian teaching, or heresy as a reason to scorn barbarians.[41] Ambrose is actually a case in point. He juxtaposes Julianus Valens's impiety with the shock of his parading Gothic garb in front of Roman troops (doubtless, in fact, barbarians in Roman service), but the impiety is Gothic "gentile" idolatry, not heresy. Non-Nicenes can comment, just like pro-Nicenes, on barbarian savagery, and when Ambrose claims—to Maximinus's fury—that the breaking of faith with God has led to the cross-Danubian invasion, he does not conflate the "sacrilegious voices" of the heretics with the "barbarian movements" of the Goths.[42] He would have had little reason to do so. As any Western pro-Nicene knew, "Arianism" had gained its currency among the Goths, precisely because it had been championed so steadfastly by churchmen on the Roman side of the Danube frontier.[43]

As often, ancient writers are the shrewdest guides to their own times. Consideration of Wulfila's creed and the extant Gothic texts decisively rules out an old scholarly belief, shaped by modern German nationalism, in a distinctive "Germanic Arianism." The theology accepted by Wulfila and the non-Nicenes of the post-Roman kingdoms was Latin Homoianism, of the kind we will explore further in the next chapter.[44] Theology *in Gothic* was subtly different. Gothic writing appears largely to be a product of Wulfila's own heyday, and so reflects aspects of Eusebian thinking current before the theological realignments of the late 350s and 380s. Either way, later Germanic Homoianism was, on a doctrinal level, just non-Nicene Christianity, and fully continuous with currents within the churches of the Roman Empire. This means that we cannot describe the ways in which Christian teaching may have been accommodated to the cultural sensibilities of the Germanic-speaking peoples, beyond Philostorgius's unverifiable claim that Wulfila refused to inflame a warlike people by translating the books of Kings.[45] It also means something more positive for historical analysis: We can draw on all of the later Homoian texts together, without having to worry that some represent the parochial views of peoples who did not understand the tradition they had embraced.

# Part IV

# Non-Nicene Thought After 381

CHAPTER 9

# Later Homoian Theology

A STUDENT OF the Arian controversy could easily suppose that non-Nicene Christianity is an evidentiary iceberg. For six decades, every scrap of information is weighed and weighed again. The two centuries of "Arian" history from the 380s to 589 float, invisible, below the theological waterline. The reason is not, in fact, a lack of data—not in comparison with the early Homoians or Arius himself. In addition to Philostorgius's Eunomian *Ecclesiastical History* in Byzantine Greek paraphrase, we have Latin Homoian sermons, theological and polemical treatises, arguments presented in live debate with Augustine, and commentaries on Luke (quite fragmentary) and the opening chapters of Job, not to mention the gigantic *Incomplete Commentary on Matthew*, which was hugely popular, under a mistaken attribution to John Chrysostom, in the Middle Ages.[1]

Why the later "Arians" vanish is a subtler problem. Frankly put, they are less stimulating for modern theologians than their forebears. Homoian thought follows the pattern apparent, in the 380s, from Auxentius's letter on Wulfila. Studying later Homoian theology is a project in nuance, not in bold new ideas. Moreover, both Homoian and Eunomian Christianity became historical dead ends. No living tradition descends from the non-Nicene churches, and so their contribution to Christian dogmatic development was largely complete by the 380s. Unsurprisingly, the later "Arians" become a niche concern within Patristics.[2]

That, we think, is a missed opportunity. In the later non-Nicenes, we finally have a chance to see the other side: what non-Nicenes made of the theological figures modern Patrologists have labored to excavate out of pro-Nicene accounts; how non-Nicene distinctives shaped the theology presented to ordinary laity; and how Homoian thought actually related to the questions of philosophy and theological method broached by the creeds of the late 350s. Issues of history and tradition are richly attested, from a chiefly Eunomian perspective. We will give them the whole of chapter 10. Now, we turn to the theology of the later Homoians, in two senses: how it was communicated, from day to day, in their churches, and how Latin writers continued to advance and develop the truths (for so they saw them) that had been cemented at the great councils of Rimini and Seleucia, under the reign of St. Constantius.

## Church Life and Preaching Among the Later Latin Homoians

One key fact conditions the study of later Latin Homoianism. Without being distinctively un-Roman, Homoianism became the theology of churches linked to the Germanic barbarians and their kings.[3] Scholarly study of the Western Homoian churches tends to focus on politics and ethnic identity, since tension and coexistence between the western Romans and their new, Germanic overlords are central questions in the transition from antiquity to the Middle Ages. In North Africa, the Vandal kings tried to force consensus around the creed of Rimini, provoking numerous pro-Nicene polemical works. In Ostrogothic Italy, Theoderic practiced a benevolent toleration, until almost the end of his reign. In Spain and Aquitaine, the Visigothic kings sought to maintain a separation between their people and the local Romans, but ultimately destroyed their "Arian" books upon official conversion at the Third Council of Toledo in 589—a disastrous impediment to saying much about their churches.[4]

Royal policy shaped churchly life and still shapes the historical information available to us. Ethnicity and language certainly mattered, too. Gothic liturgy, still in use in Byzantine churches in the Crimea in the eighth or ninth century, is attested in North Africa in the late fifth.[5] In Italy, Theoderic and his court built an aura of prestige around their Gothic heritage. They commissioned Gothic biblical codices such as the *Codex Argenteus*, a deluxe manuscript with gold and silver letters on imperial purple vellum.[6] They invented an ancient lineage for his dynasty, the Amals.[7] They supported the scribes who copied the *Skeireins* and wrote the Bologna fragments (chapter 8). Our only trace of Gothic preaching, this document is our best indication that Gothic was still in routine churchly use. It looks more like a preacher's notes than a careful composition fit for a grand state occasion (Christmas or Easter, say, in the church of a great Christian king, with the glorious purple gospel book ready for reading). In theology and church art, however, as in law, literature, and bureaucracy, the idiom of high culture was Roman. Theoderic's palace church is a good example. Rededicated by pro-Nicenes to the anti-Arian St. Martin of Tours in 561 and now known as Sant'Apollinare Nuovo, the palace church of Ravenna was decorated with mosaics in good late Roman style. Nothing on them is markedly Homoian, though a key pro-Nicene addition—a sequence of saints headed by St. Martin—certainly could have replaced a Gothic set of worthies.[8]

Like the original decoration of Sant'Apollinare Nuovo, many ritual details one would like to know are now beyond recovery. Take hymnody. No reports indicate whether local Homoian congregations chanted songs (Gothic or Latin) to reinforce their theological claims, as Ambrose's pro-Nicene congregation had done during mass "sit-ins" at Milan in 385–86 and as Homoians had done at Constantinople down to about 400.[9] So far as the Homoian churches themselves go, however, every indication is that the symbiosis of Gothic and Latin continued. Equally evident is a basic fact, too easily forgotten amid academic reconstruction of "Arian" particulars: In most aspects of churchly life, Homoians had not diverged from the Christian mainstream.

Sermons are the only element of the ancient Homoian liturgies that are genuinely well attested. Apart from the Bologna fragment, Gothic preaching is entirely lost. Latin sermons survive in two manuscripts. One is an eighth-century codex, likely of French origin, that is held at Munich.[10] Its contents are mostly pro-Nicene, but twelve sermons seem to be the work of a nameless Homoian preacher, whose Latin biblical text reveals knowledge both of the Greek and of Wulfila's Gothic version. He may have been preaching in Illyricum, south of the Danube, and not in one of the later barbarian kingdoms.[11] The sermons pertain to crucial churchly seasons: Christmas, Epiphany, Lent, and Passiontide. The concluding doxologies are non-Nicene, glorifying God the Father, generally "through" the Son and "in" the Holy Spirit. Both Christology and Trinitarian thought are likewise Homoian: Christ is the "only-begotten God," begotten of the Father and subsisting beforehand only in his "will, foreknowledge, and power."[12] By no means equal to the "invisible Father," he is no "mere man" either, but God in the flesh.[13] The preacher insists, against the "heretics," that Christ did not take on a human soul and that Father, Son, and Holy Spirit cannot be equal or have "one substance."[14]

From these convictions, the preacher constructs an explanation for Christ's incarnation. The need for a body lay in the inability of human eyes to "contemplate the naked form of the only-begotten God" directly, rather than in his own inability to relieve human sins without it. The power to forgive sins belongs, after all, to God and not to the body.[15] Christ, on the cross, bound the strong man, the devil.[16] Salvation is, it seems, a work of Christ's deity; his humanity is but a bodily instrument. Despite the clear disagreement with pro-Nicenes, the preacher's soteriology still rests upon common Christian convictions. The only-begotten God, our Lord, the Wisdom of God, really did became incarnate; he was born of a virgin; his birth was decreed before the ages; and so on. This soteriology also intersects with shared sacramental practices. In his baptism, "Jesus sanctified water, summoned the apostles, exalted the church, gave the adoption of sons, showed the doorway to eternal life—in order to make people worthy of life and the kingdom of heaven."[17] "Righteousness, piety, and gentleness" are the correct conduct in Lent, with fasting and prayer, not lawsuits, gossip, false witness, curses, and lies.[18] Any pro-Nicene churchman would have heartily agreed, just not on the church in which to get baptized or in which to hold one's fast. Rites, texts, theological premises, and holidays are shared; key theological conclusions, and the churchly community that held them, set the Homoians apart.

The other homiletic collection is a late fifth- or early sixth-century codex held at Verona.[19] This remarkable book opens with a fragmentary treatise on the names of the apostles, translated badly from Greek. Sermons on gospel readings follow. The doxologies are again "Arian," but one of the sermons is a selection from Augustine's *Expositions of the Psalms*, and the rest could have begun pro-Nicene, as well. Bits from Jerome's translation of Eusebius's gazetteer of biblical place names follow. A second collection of sermons then treats festal days. The preacher is obviously familiar with the first collection, and his Trinitarian theology, though Homoian, remains a secondary theme. The days and saints are universal: major church holidays (Christmas, Epiphany, etc.), the Holy Innocents, Stephen, John the Baptist, Peter and Paul, Cyprian of Carthage, and all the martyrs together. Not one reference is made to parochial Gothic figures. After the sermons come three polemical works, against Jews, pagans (in two rather different copies, one incomplete and set off by more from the Eusebian gazetteer), and heretics. Those are Homoousians, attacked with full vigor and in terms reminiscent of the Munich preacher's. The work lacks a title and is oddly brief, but the opening, beginning with Christ's authority as teacher, reads like a plausible start to a theological argument and a closing doxology implies that the scribe thought he had the complete ending, at any rate. The codex concludes with a sermon from Augustine (350), anonymized and wrapped up with another Arian doxology, and a long chunk from the *Apostolic Constitutions*, a model for church order by a probably Eunomian writer active ca. 360.[20]

The Verona codex is a compendium of practical Christian knowledge. Like the Munich preacher, the churchmen responsible for it were perfectly capable of polemic, and knew their Homoian doctrine. Like him, however, they expressed that doctrine within a matrix of standard Christian teaching: about the holy days of the church, the scriptures, the lives and works of the saints, proper church order, and tools for exegesis; about salvation and Christ's descent into Hell; and about God and the nature of Christ. Only on these last but central topics did they express a distinctive doctrine, which also shaped the Munich preacher's view of salvation. Like the preaching of Augustine, John Chrysostom, and other pro-Nicenes, their sermons were an expression, first, of the common "mere Christianity" of late antiquity and, secondarily, of a specific tradition developing amid heresy and schism.

## Developments in Later Homoian Theology

To grasp that tradition, we have several texts on which to draw: the short theological exposition preserved by Augustine as the *Sermon of the Arians*, the commentaries, and several polemics. This last set includes Maximinus's debate with Augustine, his introduction to Palladius's counterblast to Ambrose, the brief anti-Nicene treatise from the Verona codex, and two works—one a kind of catechesis, the other an argument against pro-Nicene theologians—preserved in the same rewritten manuscript from Bobbio in Italy that contains the *Skeireins*.[21] The writers of these works were active from the 380s onward, with several clearly living under Roman rule. References to the ascendancy of heretics abound, especially in the *Unfinished Commentary on Matthew*, whose author was familiar with Constantinople and was no lover of barbarians.[22] He was a careful interpreter of scripture, aware of Jerome's commentary on Matthew and of various apocrypha.[23] His Homoian doctrines tend to come out in sudden asides, soon submerged by engagement with Matthew itself. Whoever he was, he was the outstanding theologian of the later Homoian churches. The rest are less incisive, even Maximinus, a nimble polemicist, and the Job commentator, who knew his Greek quite well.[24] Some writers were capable of strange arguments—notably, the Luke commentator, who infers from Luke 1:32, not just that Christ would be distinct from the Highest, but also that he would not be *physically* short, like Zacchaeus.[25]

Even the Luke commentator, however, does not reject philosophical vocabulary. One would expect to find the Homoians constantly attacking the language of "substance," lambasting the Nicene Creed for its use of an invented philosophical word (*homoousios*), and relying on "like" (in Latin, *similis*) to explain how the Son relates to the Father. None of these things is the case. *Similis* is no more central than it had been for Wulfila or Palladius. Not one extant homily uses it in reference to the Son's divinity. The *Sermon of the Arians* does use it, just as Palladius had, of Christ's likeness in activity and—again like Palladius and Wulfila—while also asserting the *difference* between the Father, the Son, and the Holy Spirit.[26] The Bobbio polemicist agrees, denouncing "Macedonian" belief that the Son is "like in all things" and has "no difference" with the Father alongside Homoousian belief in outright equality.[27] Maximinus puts the actual emphasis neatly: "We do not deny that the Son is like the Father."[28]

In turn, "substance" (*substantia*), banned at Rimini as unbiblical, is used without qualm in several later Homoian works. Sometimes, as usually in the *Unfinished Commentary*, it just means "wealth."[29] Elsewhere, as in Maximinus's dispute with Augustine, it refers to an essence or nature, of humanity (or the human body), angels, or divinity.[30] Maximinus was using Augustine's language, but he did not have to. Faced with an opportunity to promote the authority of the Rimini council, as he does when denying that the Son had been created *ex nihilo*, he instead explains his conviction that higher spirits cannot be discerned by lower ones (the Son sees the Father as one *incapabilis*—"beyond grasping"—yet "honors him worthily").[31] A slightly chastened version of ideas once floated by Arius himself, this doctrine may not be philosophy of Augustine's caliber; but it is still philosophy.

*Substantia* is not a load-bearing element in Homoian thought. Not even Maximinus was working out a theory of how divine "substances" related. Even so, philosophical terminology evidently did not seem objectionable to Homoians. Why not? Perhaps because Latin pro-Nicenes had showed that they did not need to rely on *homoousios* to make their point. The word does come up.[32] It is joined, however, by a native Latin word, *aequalis* ("equal"), used to the exclusion of *homoousios* in the debate with Maximinus and treated by Augustine as its equivalent.[33] That made the stakes perfectly clear. Homoians and pro-Nicenes did not differ over mere words, but over the doctrine of God they expressed.

All of the later Homoian texts agree with Auxentius and Wulfila on the divine hierarchy. There are three significant developments. First, Christology. The Homoians conceive of Christ as a mighty but inferior divinity indwelling a human body directly.[34] Like the Munich preacher, the Bobbio catechist attacks outright the pro-Nicene belief in Christ's soul.[35] Others are less direct. Maximinus is especially subtle, taking pro-Nicene belief in Christ's subordination as man to refer rather to his "body" or "flesh."[36] The Matthew commentator often condemns the heretical view that Christ was "mere man" (*purus homo*)—presumably, a reductionist caricature of typical pro-Nicene Christology—and speaks of the descent of Christ's "naked divinity" into hell, to crush death, free the captives, and overwhelm the demons.[37]

Second, the doctrine of God. The term "Trinity" is found rarely, only twice in reference to the Homoians' own doctrine. The preacher of the Verona Pentecost sermon infers the "order of the Trinity" from the processions: The Son is sent by the Father, the Holy Spirit by the Son.[38] The Bobbio catechist uses it much the same way, citing 1 Corinthians 12:3, John 14:6, and Matthew 28:18–20: The Spirit magnifies the Son and the Son, the Father.[39] Others are distinctly wary. The Matthew commentator connects the "thorns" (*tribuli*) of Matthew 7:16 to the "professors of the Trinity," and later denounces those who think the martyrs confessed "a Trinity of the same substance." He does not try to reclaim the term for the doctrine of "one Unbegotten and one Only-Begotten and one Holy Spirit."[40] Fastidiosus, a North African convert to Homoianism, attacks belief in an "inseparable and undivided Trinity," likewise without overtly reclaiming the word.[41] The Job commentator takes the step outright: He denounces the "sect and heresy and infidelity of the Trinity," whose doctrine is termed in Greek "*trias* or *homoousios*."[42] In 357, "the complete, perfect number of the Trinity" had still been the capstone of the first Homoian manifesto. For some later Homoians, by contrast, the word had been irretrievably tainted by its pro-Nicene use, and seemed to conflict with the absolute supremacy of the ingenerate Father.

Third, a few authors present a sharper systematization of the hierarchical relations stated, in terms now lacunose, by Wulfila's creed. Thus, the author of the *Sermon of the Arians* asserted, with stark clarity, what the preacher of the Verona Pentecost sermon seems to imply: The Spirit is the Son's witness, servant, and worshipper, subordinate to him in a way closely analogous to the Son's subordination to the Father.[43] Others still put the stress on the Father's initiative: Thus, the Bobbio polemicist says that the Father "gave and sent the Holy Spirit" by ordering the Son to do so, and says that "all things" (clearly including the Spirit) "were created by the Father through the Son."[44] Granted that the *Sermon of the Arians* also says that the Holy Spirit was made *through* the Son,[45] we are likely dealing merely with subtly different ways of explaining a shared dogma. Such thinking may help to explain why the last committed "Arian" king in the West, the Visigoth Leovigild, floated a compromise basically identical to the old "Pneumatomachian" position. The Son could be admitted as God; but the Holy Spirit could not.[46] It was in Spain, likewise, that the phrase "and from the Son" was added to the Niceno-Constantinopolitan creed, not long after 589,[47] securing the coequal deity of all three persons in the way that Augustine had explained the Trinity.

## Conclusion

The defining strand within Homoian thought has sometimes been seen as a biblicist conservatism suspicious of higher-order reasoning.[48] Biblicism, however, is never mere biblicism: It contains assumptions about who God is, what words mean, and which unbiblical terms (*ingenitus, trinitas, homoousios*) may be used and which biblical terms (*aequalis, similis, unigenitus, substantia*) can be laden with a theological meaning the scriptures do not self-evidently accord them. So, too, exegesis that may seem woodenly literalist can express ideas of some conceptual sophistication. The Munich preacher, for example, asserts the superiority of the Father to the Son and the Son to the Holy Spirit from the inferiority of a dove to a man and a man to the invisible God.[49] He cannot mean that the Son is *just a man* or the Spirit *just a dove*, since he objects that the pro-Nicenes make the Son "mere man."[50] The logic, surely, is that the choice of a particular instrument of revelation gives privileged insight into divine realities. Scriptural language is a perspicuous window onto divine ontology.

There is a more cogent explanation for the intellectual narrowness of so much Homoian reasoning. These were minority churches, which produced at least one noteworthy exegete. They produced none of the singular geniuses who most attract historians and Patrologists. Their works reveal the ordinary churchly world beneath the level of Ambrose, Jerome, or Augustine. The Nicene Filastrius of Brescia, ally of Ambrose at Aquileia, was as biblicist and intellectually hidebound as any Homoian, and just as capable of producing arresting but inadequately developed ideas.[51] Homoians clearly did read some pro-Nicene works, and their most learned theologians appear to be aware of debates roiling the majority church.[52] However, they were cut off by conviction and church membership from the mainstream of Latin theology.[53] Pro-Nicenes were not merely winning in numbers; they were producing a theological tradition in which non-Nicenes, despite sharing scriptures, practices, and most basic beliefs, were not really part.

CHAPTER 10

# Eunomians, "Arians," and Church History

The history of the Arian controversy and thus of non-Nicene Christianity is relayed above all by pro-Nicene writers. This is true of our fourth-century sources; it is also true of the fifth-century histories that offer narratives of the controversy and preserve key fourth-century documents. Socrates, Sozomen, and Theodoret tend to cast the controversy, from its beginning, as a contest between the orthodox and the Arians. To turn, as we now do, to non-Nicene perspectives on fourth-century church history is therefore to uncover a vital control on our overarching sense of what the controversy was about. On the simplest level, examining non-Nicene historiography is another opportunity to see what non-Nicenes actually thought—about God, but also about the persons and events that had shaped the controversies through which they, too, had lived. It enables us to calibrate pro-Nicene narratives, on which we inevitably depend, against views from "the other side." It can therefore serve as a curb against an over-aggressive reading between the lines of pro-Nicene writing. Scholars have wanted, rightly, to understand thinkers such as Arius and Eunomius on their own terms. We risk starting to see pro-Nicene writers through black-tinted glasses—forgetting that their mistakes, invectives, and distortions are simply the ones we can still read, not the only ones that were committed, and not always the worst. Even more subtly, we may begin to mistake our best rationalizations of non-Nicene thinking for the non-Nicenes' actual motivation. The remnants of non-Nicene historical reflection cut against both pro-Nicene and modern perspectives: against the pro-Nicenes, by tracing alternative lines of theological authority from before the controversy's beginning to the fifth century; but against modern views, as well, by validating the pro-Nicene stress on Arius, his early supporters, and the doctrine of the Son's inferiority to the Father.

## A Different history, a Different Arianism

### *Philostorgius*

One figure is central to study of non-Nicene visions of the past. Born at Borissus in Cappadocia, Philostorgius was raised a Eunomian. He had met the elderly Eunomius at Constantinople but knew Aëtius's career only secondhand.[1] His twelve-book history drew on a range of Christian and secular sources, including a fourth-century Homoian chronicle.[2] His account comes down to us, however, only in a lengthy summary by Photius, patriarch of Constantinople in the ninth century (by which time pro-Nicene theology was the only live option), and in paraphrased chunks in other Byzantine writers. What remains runs to about one hundred and sixty pages in annotated English translation, and provides a distinctly anti-Nicene slant on the history of the fourth-century church.[3]

Philostorgius's interests were not limited to theological controversy. Extant paraphrases discuss the wonders of the Indian Ocean region, the geography of the rivers of Eden, and, most important, the apocalyptic themes through which Philostorgius understood the experiences of a small, fractious, and embattled church of true believers.[4] However, as in the pro-Nicene historians, two main arcs tie the narrative together. One follows the vicissitudes of imperial rulers and their policies. The other is the struggle between two fundamental theological factions. Where pro-Nicenes pitted an overarching Arian party—one ramified and divided over the decades—against the faithful champions of Nicene orthodoxy, Philostorgius sets *heteroousios* and its defenders against the Nicene *homoousios*. He is reading the experience of the fifth-century Eunomian church, under a dominant pro-Nicene establishment, as far back as the controversy's beginning.

The results can be jarring. Eusebius of Nicomedia and his allies, we are told, substituted *homoiousios* for *homoousios* in their subscriptions at Nicaea, while Constantine later endorsed the *heteroousios*.[5] Philostorgius repeatedly casts prominent critics of Nicaea, including the main Homoiousian and Macedonian leaders, as defenders of the *homoousios*.[6] He is not blind to reality. He does recognize that these figures defended other views, sometimes in close proximity to his aspersions on their "Homoousianism."[7] He simply is not interested in subtlety, any more than Athanasius usually had been.[8] For an ardent pro-Nicene, all the alternatives either coalesced with their view or entailed Arianism. For Philostorgius, everything that was not Heteroousian basically amounted to Homoousianism.

That view is not a precise mirror image of the post-Athanasian, pro-Nicene view: The dividing line does not split all deniers of Trinitarian equality from Nicenes, but a reductionist, lumped-together Nicenism from hardline Heteroousians. The line thus falls somewhere to the "left," as it were, of the more familiar pro-/non-Nicene split. Accordingly, Philostorgius has his own alternative grasp of the controversy's theological and church-political arc. Though he does not condemn Arius as a heretic, he does criticize him for thinking God beyond human comprehension.[9] Instead, the foremost champion of (Heteroousian) orthodoxy was Eusebius of Nicomedia. Philostorgius notes the education of Eusebius and several other defenders (as he saw them) of the Heteroousian doctrine by the exegete and martyr Lucian of Antioch.[10] That association, confirmed by Arius's letter to Eusebius, has never ceased to excite historians' speculation, but Philostorgius does not actually trace the theological line directly to Lucian himself, who figures chiefly as a martyr.[11] Much clearer is the relationship between this early generation and the next, as Philostorgius describes Aëtius's teaching by the Lucianists Athanasius of Anazarbus, Antony of Tarsus, and Leontius of Antioch (who ordained Aëtius deacon), and by Paulinus of Tyre, recipient of an extant letter from Eusebius of Nicomedia.[12] Thereafter, the heroes of orthodoxy are Aëtius himself and Eunomius, supported by churchmen such as the miracle working, missionary bishop-at-large Theophilus the Indian (perhaps, in fact, from Yemen or Socotra).[13]

In the unfolding narrative, the Homoiousians Basil of Ancyra and Eustathius of Sebaste are key enemies.[14] The Homoians play a more complex role. They were dominant when Eunomius and Aëtius split away from the mainstream church, but, precisely because he casts the adherents of *homoousios* as the core enemy, they cannot serve as a consistent foil. In fact, it is doubtful that a Homoian party appears at all in Philostorgius's account of the period, from 359 to the reign of Theodosius, in which the Homoian creed was the regnant dogma in the East. The narrative operates at a finer grain than that, centering not on the doctrinal commonalities among the churchmen who advanced the Homoian creed of Constantinople, but on their relationship with the two Heteroousian stalwarts at the heart of the Eunomian vision of the fourth-century church. Philostorgius distinguishes between Acacius of Caesarea and his colleagues—Eudoxius of Constantinople and Euzoius of Antioch—who inclined toward *heteroousios*. According to Photius, Acacius was the leading villain of the intact narrative,[15] and Philostorgius's extant criticisms bear distinct doctrinal overtones. He alleges that Acacius attacked Eudoxius before Constantius II for ordaining a protégé of Aëtius and that Acacius promoted Homoousian bishops.[16]

Eudoxius and Euzoius appear in quite a different light. Philostorgius traces out the slow sundering of relations between them and Eunomius, as the two leaders repeatedly failed to restore Aëtius after his deposition in 359/360. Association with Acacius does not directly taint them, and indeed doctrinal difference plays a minimal role. Eunomius, to Philostorgius's understanding, did declare the Son to be "like according to the scriptures," and upheld the Son's passionless begetting by the Father.[17] He was speaking in Eudoxius's own church, to his host's ardent approval; but Eunomius would not endorse the creed of Rimini/Constantinople and the condemnation of Aëtius, despite Eudoxius's urging.[18] The root of the ultimate schism with Eudoxius lay in a very personal church politics. Under the pagan emperor Julian, Aëtius was in theory restored by a small synod held at Antioch, and was in fact ordained a bishop, with Eudoxius's acquiescence, at Constantinople itself.[19] Neither prelate would fully see those actions through, and so, when Eunomius finally formed a schismatic hierarchy of his own, Eudoxius and Euzoius, like other one-time supporters, were embittered against both Aëtius and Eunomius.[20] Thus, the formation of a separate hierarchy was due to contingent circumstance, and not—on a Eunomian's own telling—to an unbridgeable difference of conviction.

Separation, however, encouraged both animosity and substantive difference. Philostorgius is fiercely negative about the later Homoian leaders in the East: Demophilus of Constantinople and Dorotheus of Antioch, who succeeded Demophilus in the Homoian bishopric at Constantinople. To win over Macedonians in Eunomius's own see at Cyzicus, these two had condemned Eunomius as a mere "Anomoian," a stereotype that Philostorgius rejects absolutely.[21] He accuses Demophilus of muddling the true teaching about Christ's body and—if a more distant source can be trusted—about his creation by God.[22] Finally, when Dorotheus is exiled from Antioch by Theodosius in 381, Philostorgius offers what amounts to a summative, and highly negative, judgment on the Homoian tradition.[23] Here, he links the rejection of *ousia* and *hypostasis* at Rimini and Constantinople to Arius's own teaching, and accuses both the heresiarch and the Homoian creed of undermining divine simplicity by asserting the ineffability of God. None of the "heresies" into which the followers of Arius split was ultimately able to explain the Son's "likeness" to the Father. Whether they saw it as likeness in foreknowledge, nature, or the power to create, all their views ultimately collapsed into the one central heresy of the fourth century: the *homoousion*.

What, then, does Philostorgius see as the division between his church and the Homoians? In the historical course of their separation, acceptance of the Rimini creed and rejection of Aëtius had gone together, but the stress lay on the latter. Their core doctrinal distinctive was not the *homoios* that has now given "the Homoians" their name, but a peculiarity that Philostorgius's early champions of the *heteroousios* had lived with, or even endorsed: the idea that the Son's begetting is unknowable. From one perspective—that implicit in Philostorgius's account, in book 2, of Arius and his Lucianist/Eusebian supporters—the "Arians" could be construed as an imperfectly orthodox element aligned with the true, Heteroousian tradition. Over time, however, that alignment had sundered. Confusion and multiplicity marked the inheritors of Arius's theology, who had rejected the truth and its defenders. The implication is stupendous, though it was foreshadowed, long before, in Aëtius's rejection of ordination by one of Arius's most loyal allies.[24] Drawn to its logical conclusion, Arius's own doctrine was, in strict Eunomian eyes, in fact Homoousian.

## The Western Homoians and the History of the Fourth-Century Church

There is no Homoian church history. To reconstruct even a shadowy outline of Latin Homoian perceptions of the past, we are reliant upon two texts. The first is the anthology produced by Maximinus, when he added his introduction and conclusion to the rebuttal of Ambrose by Palladius of Ratiaria.[25] The second are the rewritten leaves of the anti-Nicene polemic preserved at Bobbio in Italy.[26] Together, these offer nothing like Philostorgius's rereading of the church politics of the fourth century. They do yield a suggestive—and remarkably Arian—perspective on the broad arc of theological history.

Maximinus's introduction is a running elaboration on Palladius's thoughts. Palladius had objected that Ambrose ought to have drawn his "idolatry," the belief in three coequal gods, from Demetrianus.[27] Maximinus identifies Demetrianus, correctly, as an anti-Christian interlocutor of Cyprian of Carthage (martyred 258 and the preeminent Father of the pre-Nicene Latin church). He quotes a long section from Cyprian's apology *To Demetrianus*. The passage not only accuses Ambrose of continuing pagan assaults on persecuted Christians, when he insinuated that the barbarian invasions were a divine punishment for Arian impiety. It also allows Maximinus to represent his view of God as Cyprian's, before it was ever Arius's.[28] What he does with Arius himself is even more striking. Palladius had protested Ambrose's invidious linking of his party's doctrine to Arius's name, yet reiterated his scriptural defense, at Aquileia, of the profession, quoted by Ambrose from Arius's letter to Alexander, of the supremacy of "the only true God."[29] What Palladius says indirectly, Maximinus declares outright: This belief is "Arius's Christian profession according to the divine teaching."[30]

Maximinus claims that he will buttress Arius's teaching with "the professions and names" of "a great many bishops," including Theognis of Nicaea and "Eusebius the historian" (i.e., of Caesarea). The only profession he actually reproduces, however, is that of Wulfila, as relayed by Auxentius.[31] Maximinus's failure to provide other professions is tantalizing. Which texts did he have in mind? A creed of Antioch 341 is too late, unless he confused Eusebius of Caesarea with Eusebius of Nicomedia. Our best clue is offered by the Bobbio polemicist. Much of his work is taken up in theological and exegetical exposition, or in rebutting his opponents: Phoebadius of Agen (one of the last pro-Nicene holdouts at Rimini in 359), Ambrose, and Hilary.[32] In what might be a buildup to something like Palladius's accusation of pro-Nicene tritheism, he quotes an alleged letter from Constantine, which acknowledges divine wrath (or so he implies) at polytheism, and introduces a letter of Constantius, now lost, to an unidentified synod.[33] The professions of emperors friendly to his side could serve as evidence in an anti-Nicene case. So could the arguments of Arius's early supporters. He quotes an appeal to tradition, including the third-century bishop Dionysius of Alexandria, by Athanasius of Anazarbus. Said by his namesake from Alexandria to have defended Arius's belief in the *ex nihilo* creation of the Son—an extremely unusual stance—this Athanasius is no less radical here, asserting baldly (in a paraphrase of Philippians 2:6) that Christ "did not think he had equal terms with God."[34] Equally subordinationist quotations follow from Theognis of Nicaea, which assert the superiority of the unbegotten Father—and yet also the propriety of venerating the begotten Son.

These snippets of a lost polemic represent the kind of material Maximinus might have cited, had he fully worked up his exposition.

Supplemented by elements in other texts, such as Maximinus's debate with Augustine, they let us trace out a Homoian vision of the golden thread of orthodox, non-Nicene tradition. At the beginning of the arc is St. Cyprian, the most venerable of the Latin Fathers. Implicitly, the whole pre-Nicene church stands with him; one might point specifically to Dionysius or to the martyr Lucian, who was honored by the Job commentator.[35] Next come Arius and his allies, exemplified by Theognis, Eusebius of Caesarea, and Athanasius of Anazarbus. After him come the worthies named by Maximinus to Augustine: the conciliar fathers at Rimini (though Valens and Ursacius, interestingly, are nowhere mentioned by the extant Latin Homoians).[36] Spanning the gap to the 380s are the figures named in the texts interwoven with Maximinus's own: Palladius, Wulfila, Auxentius of Milan, Demophilus, and Auxentius of Durostorum—virtually a who's-who of stalwart Homoianism, from Constantinople westward.[37]

Latest come, implicitly, the polemicists themselves. The Bobbio polemicist might have been writing as early as the 380s,[38] and could be one of the Homoian churchmen known to us. Maximinus was writing no earlier than the promulgation of the *Theodosian Code* in 438, in a Latin world increasingly barbarian and so, despite his antipathy for the conquerors, also increasingly Homoian.[39] The shift in church politics has allowed a new openness about the continuity of Homoian conviction with its early fourth-century predecessors. In 427, while safe beneath the aegis of the Roman general Sigisvult, Maximinus could publicly expound the theology of his church; but he also reminded Augustine of the tortures a hostile imperial establishment could visit upon him for his fidelity.[40] In the 440s, there was no need to foreground the risk of persecution, and no need to dissemble any longer. His church was not "Arian." The continuity (as Maximinus saw it) with Cyprian proved that. Arius, however, had been a genuine spokesman for the true doctrine of God, which the Nicenes had rejected and Palladius had so gloriously upheld beneath their treacherous onslaught.

## The Legacy of a Fourth-Century Schism
### *Homoians and Eunomians*

A modern reader need no more agree with Maximinus's claim to be continuing the teaching of Arius than his claim to be continuing Cyprian's. Despite genuine overlap, including the divine unknowability that so troubled Philostorgius,[41] the fine details of Arius's own doctrine, as set out in the *Thalia* fragments (chapter 2), really do differ from later Latin Homoianism. The contrast between Maximinus's attitude toward Arius and Philostorgius's is revealing nonetheless, and all the more so because of mutual silence: The Western Homoians are a signal gap in Philostorgius's *dramatis personae*, and the Eunomians in Western Homoian perceptions of the heretical field.

Philostorgius knows that the Constantinople Creed was first promulgated at Rimini, and tells how accession to the Western creed was demanded of Eunomius, alongside ratification of Aëtius's deposition.[42] Following Constantinople 360, doctrinal statement and church-political maneuver formed a package deal. In the attack on Arius and his modern followers, Philostorgius also voices doctrinal concerns over the creed, as we have seen. However, Philostorgius seems not to have criticized, and maybe not have known much about, the Latin-speaking allies of Eudoxius, Euzoius, and Acacius. Only two are named: the now-obscure Domninus of Marcianopolis and "a certain Valens," who interceded for Eunomius when he was exiled in 366 and turned up at Mursa.[43] Per Photius's summary, Philostorgius gives no sign that he realized that this defender of Eunomius was in fact the foremost architect of the settlement at Rimini.

That is a telling omission, since Philostorgius might reasonably have inferred that sympathy with the *heteroousios* extended beyond Eudoxius and Euzoius to the Western Homoian leadership. Here—at least if we can trust Photius's summary as it has been transmitted—we run into a serious puzzle. Philostorgius lauds Wulfila for his work as a translator and claims that both he and his successors (literally, "those under him") held to Heteroousian orthodoxy.[44] We know, however, that this cannot have been the case, and that Philostorgius ought to have realized it. Both the Eunomian and the Arian communities of Constantinople had splintered repeatedly over doctrinal and disciplinary differences.[45] The Goths around Wulfila's successor, Selenas, had embraced the belief that the Father was always Father, even before the Son's begetting.[46] That conviction is at odds with Eunomian orthodoxy. Philostorgius, resident at Constantinople, might not have known or believed that Wulfila had taught the ineffability of God. He has, however, to have known of local Gothic support for the doctrine for which he had earlier faulted the eminent Eusebian Theognis of Nicaea.[47] Why, then, does he appear to praise not just Wulfila but also his successors?

Philostorgius's attitude is matched by Homoian silence about the Eunomians. The one condemnation comes in a live debate with Augustine. His "Arian" disputant, the imperial count Pascentius, condemned both Arius and Eunomius, and demanded that Augustine condemn the *homoousion* in turn.[48] Pascentius could not have seen either theologian as a pillar of true doctrine, but he was not making a considered judgment on Eunomius's theology, either. That we receive only from the *Unfinished Commentary on Matthew*, and only on a peripheral point: Eunomius's teaching that Joseph consummated his marriage with Mary.[49] The commentator is incensed, but he does not accuse Eunomius of heresy or even bring up his doctrine of God, which the same discourse, according to Philostorgius, had discussed.[50]

What is going on here? Do we have proof that the sundered wings of the old non-Nicene alliance drew back together, as the 380s receded into memory—proof that all were really united as "Arians" in the end? Certainly not from Philostorgius's perspective, and not in church-political fact: Even the so-called Psathyrian schism, among the Homoians at Constantinople, over the Fatherhood of God lasted decades, until 419.[51] Philostorgius was writing after a schism in his own church, at around the same time, over the claims to authority by Eunomius's nephew.[52] In Constantinople, the only Eastern city where we can see them in any detail, the non-Nicenes were as fractious as any small denomination nowadays. Generations later, in the West, Roman legal experts compiling a law code for the Visigothic king Alaric II (d. 507) could take over an imperial law on heresies without excising (or emphasizing) its anti-Eunomian language.[53] A Homoian king was not conscious of kinship with the Eunomians, any more than his churchmen were conscious of special hostility.

Most likely, what we are seeing on both sides is a chance harmonization of personal distance and theological similarity. When he lauds Wulfila's heirs, Philostorgius can only mean the Western, Latin- and Gothic-speaking barbarians. If his grasp of their teaching was shaky, so, surely, was that of his local opponents. They could safely be invoked to show that the *heteroousios*, despite the Empire's failures, still enjoyed a wider support. For staunch Homoians, meanwhile, the differences with the Eunomians had always been more political than doctrinal, acutely though a Eunomian diehard might detest divine ineffability. For Latin churchmen, even if they visited Constantinople, the politics mattered little from day to day, since the Eunomians had never become established outside the Greek-speaking world. Thus, we are presented with a remarkable result: As the non-Nicene churches fade from clear historical sight, they resolve simultaneously into a mess of competing factions and a broad theological détente.

# Conclusion

IT HAS BEEN said that scholars can be divided into "lumpers" and "splitters."[1] In fact, the crucial challenge in writing intellectual history is to integrate an appreciation for genuine continuity and similarity with the sharp individuality of past personalities and movements. Owed ultimately to the arguments of Eustathius of Antioch in the 320s and Athanasius from the 330s onward, the traditional concept of "Arianism" is aggressively reductionist. It aims not to understand the thinking of those labeled "Arian," but to show it tantamount to Arius's ideas and thus wrong, per a theological standard anchored at Nicaea in 325. The scholarship of the last four decades has sought to get the peculiarities of each ancient position—ideally, each individual theologian—into ever-sharper focus. Many have continued to stress the similarities among Arius's allies, or between Eunomians and Homoians. The overall result, however, has been the dissolution of the old sense of continuity across the whole of non-Nicene theology. "Arianism" has been placed firmly in scare quotes. The differences are now more salient than the commonalities.

In our own narrative, we have more often followed those who see residual similarities, between Arius and his early allies, between the later configurations of subordinationist theology and the earlier, or between the divided branches of non-Nicene thought after the 380s, than those who would draw sharp ruptures across the wider trajectory. We, too, would continue to place "Arianism" in scare quotes, since no one did straightforwardly accept, or develop, the propositions Arius lays out in the *Thalia*. After all, if the Homoians had won out, would we classify Augustine (or Basil of Caesarea, or Marcellus of Ancyra) as an Athanasian?[2] Possibly, in recognition of Athanasius's fame—and yet the term would not achieve the degree of resolution that serious historical and theological study both demand. It would just be a shorthand for "proponent of Trinitarian equality." "(Pro-)Nicene" will do better; and so better to call the *opponents* of Trinitarian equality, just as simply, "anti-Nicenes" or "non-Nicenes."

Here, however, we run into one of the knottiest difficulties in study of the controversy. The dividing axis of pro-Nicene versus anti-Nicene applies well at the end, to one looking backward along two trajectories (or three, if the Macedonians, by upholding the Son's coequal deity yet not the Holy Spirit's, count as a "third way"). Each trajectory is ramified and divided, but each is also still broadly coherent. Prolonged argument and external pressure had exercised a clarifying effect. Sometimes, they revealed commonalities hitherto masked by animosity: what seems to have happened, in the late 350s and 360s, between Homoiousians and pro-Nicenes, as the former moved toward a Nicene view of the Son but continued to question the full deity of the Holy Spirit. Sometimes, the clarification cemented ever-deeper differences. That, in relation to the now-dominant Nicenes, is what happened with both the Homoians and the Eunomians, whose own differences had been made acutely salient by their failure to maintain organizational and ritual unity in the 360s.

The axis pro- versus anti-Nicene is also a plausible dividing line at the controversy's beginning. The original creed of Nicaea was formulated to exclude Arius and his most loyal allies. This small cadre were the original "non-Nicenes," virtually by definition. A broader group was able to acquiesce to the council's creed, yet manifestly disagreed with its church-political outcome, and thus about the underlying theological conviction. Arius's alleged errors, in these churchmen's eyes, were neither fatal nor the most important aspect of his theology. The difficulty, then, is that the division along Nicene lines is nowhere near as salient in the interim, between Arius's death in 336 or, at latest, the Council of Antioch of 341 and the late 350s. Here, we have the ascendency of a theology that could reasonably be seen, by many later churchmen, as the genuine forebear of precisely that Homoiousian branch of non-Nicene thought that became most amenable to the pro-Nicenes. However, the theology of Antioch 341 was shaped by one of Arius's early supporters, the layman Asterius. It was configured against Marcellus of Ancyra, whose treatise *Against Asterius* had been answered by Eusebius of Caesarea, who had also been a supporter of Arius in the 320s. The conciliar theology had likewise been accepted, before his death in 341, by Arius's leading supporter, Eusebius of Nicomedia (now bishop of Constantinople). Antioch 341 was still substantially the work of members of the early pro-Arian alliance. Is the center of resistance to Nicaea to be found here, in a relatively moderate opposition both to Marcellus and to Arius's most provocative ideas, or in the continuity, recognized by later radicals, back to the equally rigorous subordinationists of the early 320s?

In the narrative that we have drawn, we have followed the cue of the later non-Nicenes, without neglecting the perspective of the less radical Homoiousians. The alternative approach is rationally coherent. One could see Homoian and Homoiousian thought alike as evolutions of the doctrine of Antioch 341. Some scholars have pointed in that direction, with solid primary evidence to support the interpretation: The first Homoian manifesto, in 357, was the work of longtime Eusebians, who certainly did incorporate elements of the Antiochene creedal tradition into their new statement. We do not believe, however, that such a narrative can adequately account for the shared subordinationism of both the earliest and the late Homoians. Moreover, the man-to-man chain of tradition that links Arius's early supporters to the Heteroousians around Aëtius demonstrates that a strong ontological subordinationism did not simply disappear in the late 330s.

In that light, the best explanation for the eclipse of hard subordinationism in the 340s and 350s may lie in the nature of the evidence. In those years, our grasp of "Eusebian" theology is limited, almost exclusively, to conciliar documents: creeds and the like. Apart from the fragments of Theodore of Heraclea, we have very little developed theology. Even Theodore's works are exegetical, not polemical, and filtered, except (presumably) for the scraps extant in the Gothic *Skeireins*, by later pro-Nicene scribes. Naturally, one reads both Theodore's fragments and the creeds in light of the nearest available, intact comparanda: Eusebius of Caesarea's *Against Marcellus* and *On Ecclesiastical Theology* (themselves written in a tradition continued by the likewise fragmentary work of his successor Acacius). One cannot do anything else, unless we choose simply to take Athanasius at his polemical word: no safer than trusting a White Russian émigré to explain, in the heat of argument, what Molotov or Trotsky claimed to believe. We have no way, however, to assess what Valens and Ursacius, the teachers of Aëtius, or his sometime-ally Eudoxius actually thought—let alone what was held by a true, original ally of Arius, such as Euzoius. These men may always have differed as sharply on the details from, say, Basil of Ancyra, as did the pro-Homoiousian Hilary of Poitiers from the (to his opponents) apparently modalist Marcellus. It simply took the destruction of the Eusebian creedal consensus, at the hands of Aëtius's supporters in the East and Valens and Ursacius in the West, to make the differences clear. Things, as a man once said, are always hardening to a point. It may just take many years for them to do so.

That hardening took place in a large part through rejection of Nicaea and the formulation of an alternative creed, the Homoian formula of 359–360. Even so, the two main theological trajectories were not differentiated exclusively through explicit creedal formulation. No conciliar standard ever seems to have served as a litmus or shibboleth for the Eunomians. Likewise, while the Homoians consistently proffered the Rimini council as a standard, they articulated theologies of a subordinationist character much more specific than the literal wording of the Homoian creed required. Nicaea, accepted or rejected, was thus the crucial touchstone on all sides.

Even its supporters, however, never reduced their practical and constructive theology to simple exposition or elaboration of a dogmatic formula, whether the original creed of Nicaea 325 or the revisions from Constantinople 381. For decades, the defenders of the equality of Father, Son, and Holy Spirit conducted their arguments largely without reference to the Nicene creed or its most distinctive clause, the *homoousion*. Refutation of the Pneumatomachians required decisive extension beyond the literal wording of Nicaea (hence, in fact, much of the language added in 381). In the West, debate often proceeded with Nicaea as a touchstone, but in direct reference not to "consubstantiality" but to the idea of "equality" that the adjective *homoousios* encapsulated in one pithy, theologically productive, but controversial quasi-philosophical formulation. What was true of polemic was also true of the communication of Christian doctrine to ordinary people. Pro-Nicene sermons did regularly denounce Arians, but the Nicene Creed took centuries to enter use as a baptismal or liturgical formula, and was always supplemented, in the West, by the interrelated baptismal formulas from which the so-called Apostles' Creed derives.[3] Those were scarce less bland than the Homoian creed itself, and certainly did not rule out non-Nicene conceptions of God. What did rule them out was the articulation of robustly Trinitarian, coequalist theologies, generally in reference to the theological authority of Nicaea, often in connection to its precise wording, that nonetheless did not rest merely upon the language of shared *ousia*. The substance of theology, and not just its form, were decisive for the ancient controversy.

In recognizing that the Father, as Father, imparts his complete and undivided deity to those who can in truth be called his Son and Spirit, in acknowledging that the Son and Holy Spirit must therefore possess all the power and attributes of God without multiplication or diminution, in showing that all three Trinitarian persons must be *God* in the strict sense, pro-Nicene theologians secured, in its fulness, a key, perhaps *the* key, biblical truth. This is the fact that, though his power is often veiled in weakness, the sovereign Creator, the Lord of all that exists, is really present and active for his people's salvation within the order of the world that we see with our own eyes. The Son who became man—the man whose life, death, and resurrection were related by his followers in the gospels—is God: not a secondary, created God, not an image of the Father's will or activity, but the exact image, the eternal, begotten reality, of what the Father *is*. So, in a way more mysterious, is the Holy Spirit, who indwells all true Christians within the holy church, throughout the world. He takes from what belongs to Jesus

Christ and gives to his followers; and Jesus has both received all things from his Father and been exalted, as one God-man, to the right hand of the majesty on high. To enable and encourage the proclamation of these scriptural revelations, a true article on which the Christian faith stands or falls, was the great contribution to the unfolding of Christian theology by those ancient theologians who insisted, instead, upon the sole majesty of the Father. They encouraged Nicene theology by denying it; yet, by insisting upon the transcendent greatness of true deity, they unwittingly ensured that only a theology of coequality, one that would admit no half levels of Godhood, could endure. Christian theology, in all its forms, has often owed such clarifications to those whose teaching it has ultimately rejected.

# NOTES

## NOTE ON SOURCES

1 Further information can be found in handbooks such as the *Patrology* by Johannes Quasten, vols. 1–3 (Utrecht: Spectrum, 1949–60) and Angelo di Berardino, vol. 4 (Westminster, MD: Christian Classics, 1986): now rather outdated but still a useful first stop. Likewise valuable, and especially comprehensive, is the open-access database of "keys" to premodern Christian literature maintained by Brepols (Turnhout, Belgium), Clavis Clavium, https://clavis.brepols.net/clacla/Default.aspx, accessed September 3, 2024.

2 *Epitome of the Ecclesiastical History of Philostorgius, compiled by Photius, Patriarch of Constantinople*, trans. Edward Walford (London: Henry G. Bohn, 1855), https://www.tertullian.org/fathers/philostorgius.htm, accessed September 3, 2024.

## INTRODUCTION

1 For more on what we mean by "hard" or "strict" (i.e. *ontological*) subordinationism, see pp. 26–27.

## CHAPTER 1: BEFORE ARIUS

1 Cf. Michel René Barnes, *Augustine and Nicene Theology: Essays on Augustine and the Latin Argument for Nicaea* (Eugene, OR: Cascade Books, 2023), 123. Augustine, *De trinitate* 5.8.10, Jerome, *Epistula* 15.3–4.

2 *Power* is more important for many Latin writers than *substance*: Barnes, *Augustine and Nicene Theology*, 85–124.

3 Further discussion at pp. 107–108.

4 Origen, *Contra Celsum* 5.59.

5 Athanasius, for example, omits the deuterocanonical books of the Old Testament, except Baruch, and classes Wisdom, Ben Sira (Ecclesiasticus),

Esther, Judith, Tobit, the *Didache*, and the *Shepherd* of Hermas as useful but non-canonical (*Epistula festalis* 39). Eusebius of Caesarea, *Historia ecclesiastica* 3.3.5, 3.25.3–4, notes doubts over Hebrews, James, Jude, 2 Peter, 2 and 3 John, and Revelation.

6 For a similar point, see Lewis Ayres, *Nicaea and Its Legacy: An Approach to Fourth-Century Trinitarian Theology* (Oxford: Oxford University Press, 2004), 33.

7 A classic statement in Augustine, *De consensu evangelistarum* 1.1.1–6.9.

8 Translations follow the Greek of the Septuagint (LXX) or the New Testament, in standard modern editions: *Septuaginta, Id est Vetus Testamentum graece iuxta LXX interpretes*, ed. Alfred Rahlfs, 2nd ed., ed. Robert Hanhart (Stuttgart: Deutsche Bibelgesellschaft, 2006); *Nestle–Aland Novum Testamentum Graece*, ed. Barbara Aland, Kurt Aland, Johannes Karavidopoulos, Carlo M. Martini, and Bruce M. Metzger, 28th rev. ed., gen. ed. Holger Strutwolf, Institute for New Testament Textual Research, University of Münster (Stuttgart: Deutsche Bibelgesellschaft, 2012), both accessible through the website of the Deutsche Bibelgesellschaft, https://www.die-bibel.de/. The Septuagint often differs from the Hebrew texts on which modern translations are primarily based.

9 The Greek lacks the second "our."

10 Thus an early second-century testimony from a Roman governor: Pliny, *Epistula* 10.96 to the emperor Trajan.

11 Points well stressed by Marcia L. Colish, *The Stoic Tradition from Antiquity to the Early Middle Ages*, vol. 2, *Stoicism in Christian Latin Thought through the Sixth Century*, 2nd ed., Studies in the History of Christian Thought 35 (Leiden: Brill, 1990), 9–29 (Tertullian); Mark Julian Edwards, *Origen against Plato*, Ashgate Studies in Philosophy and Theology in Late Antiquity (Aldershot: Ashgate, 2002).

12 Tertullian, *Adversus Praxean* 7.8. In fact, Tertullian says that all "substances" are corporeal: *Adversus Hermogenem* 35.2. Technical discussion in G.C. Stead, "Divine Substance in Tertullian," *Journal of Theological Studies*, n.s., 14, no. 1 (1963): 46–66.

13 Plato, *Symposium* 203a, quoted by the Middle Platonist Apuleius, *De deo Socratis* 4.6.

14 Rowan Williams, *Arius: Heresy and Tradition*, rev. ed. (Grand Rapids, MI: Eerdmans, 2001), 117–31, has a fine discussion.

15 Barnes, *Augustine and Nicene Theology*, 38 offers a brief description.

16 Tertullian, *Adversus Praxean* 27.1–3.

17 Tertullian, *Adversus Praxean* 8.5.

18 Tertullian, *Adversus Praxean* 14.3; 29.2, 6–7.

19 Tertullian, *Adversus Praxean* 9.2–3.
20 Tertullian, *Adversus Praxean* 9.3, 8.7, 30.5.
21 Tertullian, *Adversus Praxean* 2.4, 17.4.
22 Tertullian, *Adversus Praxean* 7.4.
23 Athenagoras, *Legatio pro christianis* 10.2–4.
24 Origen, *Commentarii in evangelium Joannis* 1.24.151.
25 Compare Origen, *Commentarii in evangelium Joannis* 13.21.123–25 and Tertullian, *Adversus Praxean* 7.8–9.
26 Origen, *De oratione* 15.
27 Origen, *Contra Celsum* 1.66; Origen, *Commentarii in evangelium Joannis* 1.39.291.
28 Michel René Barnes, "The Beginning and End of Early Christian Pneumatology," *Augustinian Studies* 39, no. 2 (2008): 169–86.
29 Tertullian, *Adversus Praxean* 26.3–4.
30 Barnes, *Augustine and Nicene Theology*, 46–48.

## CHAPTER 2: ARIUS

1 Socrates, 1.5.2; Athanasius, *De synodis* 15.
2 We reduce this picture of Arius—as much else in this chapter—from the penetrating monograph by Williams, *Arius*.
3 See still Timothy D. Barnes, *Constantine and Eusebius* (Cambridge, MA: Harvard University Press, 1981).
4 "Arianism" was still used by R.P.C. Hanson, *The Search for the Christian Doctrine of God: The Arian Controversy, 318–381* (Edinburgh: T&T Clark, 1988), who explores all its vast fourth-century diversity.
5 A point underscored in key modern analyses: Williams, *Arius*, 165–66; Ayres, *Nicaea*, 2; Richard Paul Vaggione, *Eunomius of Cyzicus and the Nicene Revolution*, Oxford Early Christian Studies (Oxford: Oxford University Press, 2000), 37–43.
6 Respectively, *Urk.* 1 (Epiphanius, *Panarion* 69.6, Theodoret, 1.5.1–4), *Urk.* 6 (Athanasius, *De synodis* 16.2–5; Epiphanius, *Panarion* 69.7.2–8.5), *Urk.* 30 (Socrates, 1.26.2–7, Sozomen, 2.27.6–10).
7 For a commentary on the likeliest fragments, see Winrich Löhr, "Arius Reconsidered (Part 2)," *Zeitschrift für Antikes Christentum* 10, no. 1 (2006): 121–57, at 134–50. As Williams, *Arius*, 103–4, observes, *Oratio contra Arianos* 1.5–6 makes explicit the troubling implications often latent in *De synodis* 15.
8 A conviction probably shaped by shifts in contemporary Platonist thought: Williams, *Arius*, 181–229.

9 Origen, *Commentarii in euangelium Ioannis* 1.17.102.

10 *Urk.* 4b.10 (Athanasius, *De decretis Nicaenae synodi* 35.1–21, Socrates, 1.6.4–30, Gelasius of Caesarea, *Historia ecclesiastica* 2.3.1–21).

11 *Urk.* 1.4, 6.2.

12 Williams, *Arius*, 112–15.

13 Theodosius of Philadelphia (Philostorgius, 8.3).

14 Athanasius, *Oratio contra Arianos* 1.37. Recent scholarship has tended skeptical: Ayres, *Nicaea*, 55–56 and especially David M. Gwynn, *The Eusebians: The Polemic of Athanasius of Alexandria and the Construction of the "Arian Controversy,"* Oxford Theological Monographs (Oxford: Oxford University Press, 2007), 194–97.

15 A famous attempt to ground "Arianism" in soteriological concerns (Robert C. Gregg and Dennis E. Groh, *Early Arianism: A View of Salvation* [Philadelphia: Fortress Press, 1981]) relied too much on the alleged doctrine of the Son's mutability; a parallel effort by Hanson, *Search*, 99–122, on an over-harmonized view of "Arian" sources from all phases of the controversy. Gwynn, *Eusebians*, 194–202, is rightly critical.

16 *Urk.* 6.3.

17 *Urk.* 1.2.

18 *Urk.* 1.5.

19 *Urk.* 6.5.

20 A lengthy letter of Alexander, *Urk.* 14 (Theodoret, 1.4.1–61), lays out his Trinitarian confession.

21 We build upon the careful parsing by Mark Edwards, "Is Subordinationism a Heresy?," *TheoLogica: An International Journal for Philosophy of Religion and Philosophical Theology* 4, no. 2 (2020): 69–86, at 69–70.

22 *Urk.* 14.44–45.

23 Manlio Simonetti, *La crisi ariana nel IV secolo*, Studia Ephemeridis "Augustinianum" 11 (Rome: Institutum Patristicum "Augustinianum," 1975), 58–59.

24 Despite Athanasius, *Oratio contra Arianos* 1.5, Arius does not appear, per *De synodis* 15, to have objected to calling God "Father" in his eternal singularity (Löhr, "Arius Reconsidered," 142).

25 Löhr, "Arius Reconsidered," 144, discusses some other, possible implications.

26 Williams, *Arius*, 230–31.

27 Ayres, *Nicaea*, 27.

28 *Urk.* 14.27.

29 John 1:18, quoted by Alexander, *Urk.* 14.15.

## CHAPTER 3: THE EUSEBIANS

1 Respectively, Khaled Anatolios, *Retrieving Nicaea: The Development and Meaning of Trinitarian Doctrine*, with a foreword by Brian E. Daley (Grand Rapids, MI: Baker Academic, 2011), 41–98; Ayres, *Nicaea*, 41–61; Joseph T. Lienhard, *Contra Marcellum: Marcellus of Ancyra and Fourth-Century Theology* (Washington, DC: Catholic University of America Press, 1999), 28–46. German scholars, similarly, refer to Origenist/Eusebian *Dreihypostasentheologie*: e.g., Hanns Christof Brennecke, *Studien zur Geschichte der Homöer: Der Osten bis zum Ende der homöischen Reichskirche*, Beiträge zur historischen Theologie 73 (Tübingen: J.C.B. Mohr (Paul Siebeck), 1988), 17.

2 R.P.C. Hanson, "Who Taught ἐξ οὐκ ὄντων?," in *Arianism: Historical and Theological Reassessments, Papers from The Ninth International Conference on Patristic Studies, September 5–10, 1983, Oxford, England*, ed. Robert C. Gregg, Patristic Monograph Series 11 (Philadelphia: Philadelphia Patristic Foundation, 1985), 79–83.

3 Philostorgius, 2.14; Epiphanius, *Panarion* 69.5.2.

4 *Urk.* 1.5 (Epiphanius, *Panarion* 69.6, Theodoret, 1.5.1–4), with Williams, *Arius*, 30–31, 165–67.

5 *Urk.* 7 (quotations at the Second Council of Nicaea in 787).

6 *Urk.* 3 (quotations at Nicaea II and in Eusebius, *Contra Marcellum*, 1.40–41, 57). Both letters are preserved only in (largely hostile) excerpt, and so we cannot be confident that the quotations reflect Eusebius's overall emphasis in the intact originals: Aaron P. Johnson, "Narrating the Council: Eusebius on Nicaea," in *The Cambridge Companion to the Council of Nicaea*, ed. Young Richard Kim (Cambridge: Cambridge University Press, 2021), 202–22, at 205.

7 *Urk.* 1.4–5.

8 *Urk.* 8 (Theodoret, 1.6.1–8).

9 The label "Ariomaniac" already appears in works of Eustathius of Antioch, summarized by Sophie Cartwright, *The Theological Anthropology of Eustathius of Antioch*, Oxford Early Christian Studies (Oxford: Oxford University Press, 2015), 33–74.

10 *Urk.* 22 (Athanasius, *De decretis Nicaeni synodi* 33, Socrates, 1.8.35–54, Theodoret, 1.12, Gelasius of Caesarea, *Historia ecclesiastica* 2.35).

11 Cf. Hanson, *Search*, 197–98.

12 *Urk.* 24 (Athanasius, *De decretis* 37).

13 Constantine, *Urk.* 27.15–16 (letter to the Nicomedians; Athanasius, *De decretis* 41, Gelasius of Caesarea, *Historia ecclesiastica* 3, appendix 1), with Hanson, *Search*, 173, and Sozomen, 1.21.3–4.

14 Events described in Timothy D. Barnes, *Athanasius and Constantius: Theology and Politics in the Constantinian Empire* (Cambridge, MA: Harvard University Press, 1993), 20–25.
15 Athanasius, *Epistula ad Serapionem de morte Arii* (printed in Nicene and Post-Nicene Fathers as *Letter* 54).
16 2 Macc 9 (Antiochus Epiphanes), Acts 12:23 (Herod Agrippa I); more nearly contemporary, Lactantius, *De mortibus persecutorum* 33 (the persecuting emperor Galerius, d. 311).
17 Key historical details are contradictory: See Hanson, *Search*, 265 and Williams, *Arius*, 80–81, who deems Athanasius's story "melodramatic semi-fiction."
18 Barnes, *Athanasius and Constantius*, 1–9 assesses the problems.
19 Gwynn, *Eusebians*, presents the most thoroughgoing case.
20 Full discussion in Cartwright, *Eustathius*, esp. 75–139.
21 Cartwright, *Eustathius*, 20–31, 62–65.
22 Hanson, *Search*, 274–84.
23 Ayres, *Nicaea*, 105–6 is judicious.
24 Matthew R. Crawford, "On the Diversity and Influence of the Eusebian Alliance: The Case of Theodore of Heraclea," *Journal of Ecclesiastical History* 64, no. 2 (2013): 227–57.
25 As a papyrus letter attests: Hanson, *Search*, 252–54.
26 For a defense, Timothy D. Barnes, review of *Eusebians* by David M. Gwynn, *Journal of Theological Studies* 58, no. 2 (2007): 715–18.
27 An assumption palpable in defenses of Arius or his allies: e.g., Colm Luibheid, "The Arianism of Eusebius of Nicomedia," *Irish Theological Quarterly* 43, no. 1 (1976): 3–23.
28 Eusebius of Caesarea, *Against Marcellus and On Ecclesiastical Theology*, trans. Kelley McCarthy Spoerl and Markus Vinzent, Fathers of the Church 135 (Washington, DC: Catholic University of America Press, 2017).
29 Mark DelCogliano, "How Did Arius Learn from Asterius? On the Relationship between the Thalia and the Syntagmation," *Journal of Ecclesiastical History* 69, no. 3 (2018): 477–92.
30 On all aspects of Marcellus's thinking, see Lienhard, *Contra Marcellum*, and cf. Sara Parvis, *Marcellus of Ancyra and the Lost Years of the Arian Controversy 325–345*, Oxford Early Christian Studies (Oxford: Oxford University Press, 2006), who offers a reconstruction especially favorable to Marcellus.
31 Quoted at *De ecclesiastica theologia* 3.4.2–3.
32 *De ecclesiastica theologia* 2.7.3, 14

33 *De ecclesiastica theologia* 1.11.4; Eusebius, *Against Marcellus,* 45–48.
34 Sozomen, 3.5.9; Hanson, *Search,* 288–90.
35 *Dok.* 41.4 (Athanasius, *De synodis* 23.2–10, Socrates, 2.10.10–18).
36 *Dok.* 41.5 (Athanasius, *De synodis* 22.3–7, Socrates, 2.10.4–8).
37 Events in Barnes, *Athanasius and Constantius,* 47–81.
38 *Dok.* 43.2.2 (Theodoret, 2.8.37–52).
39 Barnes, *Augustine and Nicene Theology,* 89–90.
40 *Dok.* 43.2.3–4.
41 *Dok.* 43.2.6–7.
42 Hanson, *Search,* 303.
43 Cf. Hanson, *Search,* 304–5.
44 Hanson, *Search,* 235–38.
45 *Dok.* 47.3 (Athanasius, *De synodis* 27.2–3, Socrates, 2.30.5–30).
46 Athanasius never quite rejected him: Epiphanius, *Panarion* 72.4.4.

## CHAPTER 4: THE HOMOIOUSIANS

1 Ayres, *Nicaea,* 138–39.
2 Sozomen, 4.12–13.
3 Philostorgius, 3.15; further discussion at p. 113.
4 E.g., Thomas A. Kopecek, *A History of Neo-Arianism,* 2 vols., Patristic Monograph Series 8 (Philadelphia: Philadelphia Patristic Foundation, 1979); Hanson, *Search,* 598–636.
5 *Dok.* 61.1 (Epiphanius, *Panarion* 76.11–12, pseudo-Athanasius, *De trinitate* 2.3); edited with English translation and notes by Lionel R. Wickham, "The *Syntagmation* of Aetius the Anomean," *Journal of Theological Studies,* n.s., 19, no. 2 (1968): 532–69, whose numbering we follow.
6 John 17:3 is cited in the benedictional thesis 37, which also references the divine name from Exodus 3:14, *ho ōn*. Cf. Brennecke *et al., Dokumente,* 3:518.
7 Thus, for Aëtius's successor Eunomius, see Richard Paul Vaggione, *Eunomius: The Extant Works,* Oxford Early Christian Texts (Oxford: Clarendon Press, 1987), 29.
8 Kopecek, *History,* 8; cf. G.L. Prestige, *God in Patristic Thought* (London: SPCK, 1952), xx.
9 *Syntagmation* 12–13.
10 *Syntagmation* 36–37.
11 *Dok.* 56.5.4 (Epiphanius, *Panarion* 73.21); Xavier Morales, "Identification de l'auteur des citations néo-ariennes dans le *Traité* de Basile d'Ancyre," *Zeitschrift für Antikes Christentum* 11, no. 3 (2008): 492–99.

12 On the invention of *homoiousios*, see p. 81. It is not used in the early "Homoiousian" texts.
13 Athanasius, *De synodis* 41, Hilary, *De synodis* (at 29–33, defending Antioch 341 itself). The Latin rhetorician and lay theologian Marius Victorinus was more hostile: *Adversus Arium* 1A.23.
14 Epiphanius, *Panarion* 73.
15 Edward Gibbon, *The History of the Decline and Fall of the Roman Empire*, vol. 3 (London: W. Strahan and T. Cadell, 1783), 341. Hanson, *Search*, 347, is duly severe: "But Gibbon could never resist sacrificing history to epigram."
16 *Dok.* 55 (Epiphanius, *Panarion* 73.2.1–11.11).
17 *Dok.* 58 (Epiphanius, *Panarion* 73.12.1–22.8).
18 Mark DelCogliano, "George of Laodicea: A Historical Reassessment," *Journal of Ecclesiastical History* 62, no. 4 (2011): 667–92.
19 *Urk.* 12–13 (Athanasius, *De synodis* 17.5–6).
20 *Urk.* 16 (Hilary, *Collectanea Antiariana Parisina* Series A VII 4).
21 Robert E. Winn, *Eusebius of Emesa: Church and Theology in the Mid-Fourth Century* (Washington, DC: Catholic University of America Press, 2011), 46–50, 152–86.
22 *Dok.* 55.2–4.
23 *Dok.* 55.6.
24 *Dok.* 55.8.
25 *Dok.* 55.6.
26 *Dok.* 55.7.
27 *Dok.* 55.8–10.
28 *Dok.* 55.11.
29 *Dok.* 55.12–14.
30 *Dok.* 55.15.
31 *Dok.* 55.16.
32 *Dok.* 55.18–22.
33 *Dok.* 55.23–25.
34 Possibly on the basis of Sirmium 351: Barnes, *Athanasius and Constantius*, 109–20; but Ayres, *Nicaea*, 135, is cautious.
35 *Dok.* 56.1 (Sozomen, 4.15.2), 56.3.3 (Hilary, *De synodis* 12–25).
36 *Dok.* 57.2 (Athanasius, *De synodis* 8.3–7, Socrates, 2.37.18–24).
37 *Dok.* 57.3 (Epiphanius, *Panarion* 73.22.5–8).
38 *Dok.* 56.2 (Hilary, *De synodis* 81).
39 *Dok.* 58.1.
40 *Dok.* 58.6. Cf. Winrich A. Löhr, "A Sense of Tradition: The Homoiousian Church Party," in *Arianism after Arius: Essays on the Development of the*

*Fourth Century Trinitarian Conflicts*, ed. Michel R. Barnes and Daniel H. Williams (Edinburgh: T&T Clark, 1993), 81–100, at 93.

41 *Dok.* 58.7.

42 Palladius, *Scholia* 54; Philostorgius, 6.1.

43 *Dok.* 58.9.

44 *Dok.* 55.24, 58.10 (we quote the text as emended by Brennecke *et al.*, but the meaning is clear regardless).

45 *Dok.* 58.12.

46 Thus Löhr, "Homoiousian Church Party," 93, and the introduction by Brennecke *et al.*, *Dokumente*, 3:426.

47 DelCogliano, "George of Laodicea," 689.

48 *Dok.* 58.6.

49 *Dok.* 58.7.

## CHAPTER 5: THE WESTERN HOMOIANS

1 Cf. Adolf Martin Ritter, "Arius redivivus? Ein Jahrzwölft Arianismusforschung," *Theologische Rundschau*, n.s., 55, no. 2 (1990): 153–87, at 173.

2 For another view, extending down to the early 400s and so overlapping with the material discussed in chapters 8 and 9, see Uta Heil, "The Homoians," in *Arianism: Roman Heresy and Barbarian Creed*, ed. Guido M. Berndt and Roland Steinacher (Farnham: Ashgate, 2014), 85–115.

3 Ancient reports are garbled at key points; for modern narratives, Barnes, *Athanasius and Constantius*, 138–39, Ayres, *Nicaea*, 133–40.

4 Hilary, *De synodis* 3, 63, names Ossius and Potamius; Phoebadius of Agen, *Contra Arianos* 3, Valens, Ursacius, and Potamius.

5 *Epistula ad episcopos Aegypti et Libyae* 7.4.

6 Philostorgius, 1.9c (Nicetas, *Thesaurus* 5.8).

7 *Dok.* 46 (*Collectanea Antiariana Parisina* B II 6; Athanasius, *Apologia secunda* 58.1–4, *Historia Arianorum* 26.3, Sozomen, 23.2–5).

8 Sulpicius Severus, *Chronica* 2.39.

9 *Dok.* 51 (Hilary, *De synodis* 11).

10 Athanasius, *De decretis Nicaeni synodi*, plausibly datable between 350 and 356 (Gwynn, *Eusebians*, 29–33), though it may also be read as a reaction to the Sirmian manifesto and its Eastern reception, and so placed ca. 357–59 (Uta Heil, ed. *Athanasius von Alexandrien, De sententia Dionysii: Einleitung, Übersetzung und Kommentar*, Patristische Texte und Studien 52 (Berlin: De Gruyter, 1999), 26–32). Western councils: *Dok.* 50.2 (Sulpicius Severus, *Chronica* 2.39), 50.5 (Hilary, *Ad Constantium* 8), with Carl Beckwith, *Hilary of Poitiers on the Trinity: From* De Fide *to*

De Trinitate, Oxford Early Christian Studies (Oxford: Oxford University Press, 2008), 43–48.

11 For further parallels to early Latin Trinitarian thought, see Hanns Christof Brennecke, "Homöismus und Logostheologie," in *Logos der Vernunft—Logos des Glaubens*, ed. Ferdinand R. Prostmeier and Horacio E. Lona (Berlin: De Gruyter, 2010), 323–38, at 334–35.

12 *Adversus Praxean* 17.4.

13 Cf. Manlio Simonetti, "Arianesimo latino," *Studi Medievali*, 3rd s. 8, no. 2 (1967): 663–744, at 674.

14 *Dok.* 57.2 (Athanasius, *De synodis* 8.3–7, Socrates, 2.37.18–24).

15 *Dok.* 59.2, 4 (Hilary, *Collectanea Antiariana Parisina* A IX 1, 3), 59.3 (anathematisms preserved in two manuscripts); Brennecke, *Studien*, 29–31.

16 Sulpicius Severus, *Chronica* 2.41.6–7.

17 *Dok.* 59.7 (Hilary, *Collectanea Antiariana Parisina* A V 3).

18 *Dok.* 59.9.1, 4 (Theodoret, 2.21.3–7). For a full account of the variations among the creeds approved at Sirmium 359, at Rimini/Nike, and by the delegates from Seleucia (pp. 64–65), see Wolfram Kinzig, *A History of Early Christian Creeds* (Berlin: De Gruyter, 2024), 307–23.

19 Sulpicius Severus, *Chronica* 2.43.1–4.

20 *Dok.* 67.1 (Hilary, *Collectanea Antiariana Parisina* A I).

21 *Dok.* 59.11 (Jerome, *Altercatio Luciferiani et Orthodoxi* 17–18). Sulpicius Severus, *Chronica* 2.43.4–44.8.

22 Jerome, *Altercatio* 19.

23 Hilary, *Collectanea Antiariana Parisina* B VIII 2.2.

24 Sulpicius Severus, *Chronica* 2.44.7, Jerome, *Altercatio* 19.

25 Yves-Marie Duval, "La 'manœuvre frauduleuse' de Rimini: À la recherche du *Liber aduersus Vrsacium et Valentum*," repr. in *L'Extirpation de l'Arianisme en Italie du Nord et en Occident. Rimini (359/60) et Aquilée (381), Hilaire de Poitiers (†367/8) et Ambroise de Milan (†397)* (Aldershot: Ashgate, 1998), 96–97.

26 *Dok.* 78.1.2 (Hilary, *Collectanea Antiariana Parisina* B V).

27 *Dok.* 78.2–3 (Hilary, *Collectanea Antiariana Parisina* A III, B VI).

28 Daniel H. Williams, "Another Exception to Later Fourth-Century 'Arian' Typologies: The Case of Germinius of Sirmium," *Journal of Early Christian Studies* 4, no. 3 (1996): 335–57, at 354–55.

29 Sulpicius Severus, *Chronica* 2.39.6.

30 *Dok.* 74.1 (Hilary, *Contra Auxentium* 13–15)

31 *Dok.* 74.2 (Hilary, *Contra Auxentium* 7–9).

32 *Dok.* 78.2.

33 The standard modern accounts are Neil B. McLynn, *Ambrose of Milan: Church and Court in a Christian Capital*, The Transformation of the Classical Heritage 22 (Berkeley: University of California Press, 1994), focused more on politics, and Daniel H. Williams, *Ambrose of Milan and the End of the Arian-Nicene Conflicts*, Oxford Early Christian Studies (Oxford: Clarendon Press, 1995), focused more on theology.
34 A partial translation in Kenneth B. Steinhauser, "The Acts of the Council of Aquileia (381 C.E.)," ed. Richard Valantasis, *Religions of Late Antiquity in Practice*, Princeton Readings in Religions (Princeton: Princeton University Press, 2000), 275–88.
35 Which is not to say that his approach exactly matches Arius's own: for example, he comes closer to affirming the Son's immortality and will call him both "good" and "powerful," without joining those adjectives to a direct affirmation of his deity (*Gesta concilii Aquileiensis* 26, 28–29, 31).
36 More on p. 000, below; Neil McLynn, "The 'Apology' of Palladius: Nature and Purpose," *Journal of Theological Studies*, n.s., 42, no. 1 (1991): 52–76.
37 Palladius, *Scholia* 54.
38 See p. 51.

## CHAPTER 6: HETEROOUSIANS

1 Sozomen, 4.22.
2 *Dok.* 60.2 (Epiphanius, *Panarion* 73.25–26, Socrates, 2.40.8–17, Athanasius, *De synodis* 29.2–9).
3 Theodoret, 2.27.10–13, Philostorgius, 4.12.
4 It is unclear whether the synodical letter to George of Alexandria, *Dok.* 62.4 (Theodoret, 2.28), dates from 359 or 360, but rejection of Aëtius was henceforth a consistent policy of the Homoians: chap. 10.
5 Sozomen, 4.24–25.
6 Anti-Marcellan fragments are preserved by Epiphanius, *Panarion* 72.6–10; Mark DelCogliano, "Eusebian Theologies of the Son as the Image of God before 341," *Journal of Early Christian Studies* 14, no. 4 (2006): 459–84. Likeness: Socrates, 2.40.33. *Homoousion*: Socrates, 3.25.14, 18.
7 Such matters dominate the foremost historical study: Brennecke, *Studien*.
8 Two important statements, attributed to Eudoxius and Athanasius's Homoian successor, Lucius, were either forged or severely doctored in transmission: Hanns Christof Brennecke, "'Apollinaristischer Arianismus' oder 'arianischer Apollinarismus': Ein dogmengeschichtliches Konstrukt? Arianische Christologie und Apollinarius von Laodicea," in *Apollinarius und seine Folgen*, ed. Silke-Petra Bergjan, Benjamin J. Gleede,

and Martin Heimgartner, Studien und Texte zu Antike und Christentum 79 (Tübingen: Mohr Siebeck, 2015), 73–92, at 88–91.

9 Vaggione, *Eunomius*, 142 n. 396; others identify the temporists as pro-Nicenes or other anti-"Arians" (e.g., Ayres, *Nicaea*, 146).

10 For texts of the intact, shorter works and a schematic of the fragments of the *Apologia Apologiae* conveyed by Gregory of Nyssa's *Contra Eunomium*, see Vaggione, *Eunomius: The Extant Works*. With our citations of *Apologia Apologiae* we include references to *Contra Eunomium* in the three-volume edition published by Lenka Karfíková, Scot Douglass, Johannes Zachhuber, Johan Leemans, Matthieu Cassin, and Miguel Brugarolas, *Gregory of Nyssa: Contra Eunomium, An English Version with Supporting Studies*, Supplements to Vigiliae Christianae 82, 124, 148 (Leiden: Brill, 2007–18).

11 Exactitude: Eunomius, *Apologia* 17; tradition: Vaggione, *Eunomius*, 45–46.

12 Eunomius, *Apologia* 4–5.

13 Basil credits it, at least by way of argument: *Adversus Eunomium* 1.4.

14 Aëtius, *Syntagmation* 5.

15 *Syntagmation* 4.

16 Eunomius, *Apologia* 8.

17 *Apologia* 11.

18 Eunomius, *Apologia* 24.

19 Eunomius, *Apologia* 9; see Andrew Radde-Gallwitz, *Basil of Caesarea, Gregory of Nyssa, and the Transformation of Divine Simplicity*, Oxford Early Christian Studies (Oxford: Oxford University Press, 2009), 97.

20 Aëtius, *Syntagmation* 16.

21 Socrates, 4.7.13–14, with Hanson, *Search*, 629, Vaggione, *Eunomius: The Extant Works*, 167–70; Philostorgius, 10.2–3 (see further, pp. 115–116).

22 *Urk.* 8.3 (Theodoret, 1.6.1).

23 Aëtius, *Syntagmation* 4; Eunomius, *Apologia* 12; Eunomius, *Apologia apologiae* 3.1 (Gregory of Nyssa, *Contra Eunomium*, 3.1.4; 3.1.7).

24 Aëtius, *Syntagmation* 8, with Wickham, "*Syntagmation*," 554–55.

25 Eunomius, *Apologia apologiae* 2.4 (Gregory of Nyssa, *Contra Eunomium*, 1.9.455).

26 Eunomius, *Apologia* 28.

27 Eunomius, *Expositio fidei* 3.

28 Eunomius, *Apologia apologiae* 3.8 (Gregory of Nyssa, *Contra Eunomium*, 3.8.5).

29 Eunomius, *Expositio fidei* 4, *Apologia* 25.

30 Eunomius, *Apologia* 25.
31 Maris: Philostorgius, 5.3; Euzoius: pp. 114–115.
32 The so-called "Exposition of Patricius and Aëtius," *Dok.* 75.1 (*Historia Acephala* 4.6); Vaggione, *Eunomius*, 283–84.
33 Further discussion, from Philostorgius's partisan hindsight, at pp. 114–116.
34 Cf. Vaggione, *Eunomius*, 285–88.
35 The parallelism with the Decadents, foregrounded in these terms by Hanson, *Search*, 584, and Vaggione, *Eunomius*, 253, is hard to pass up.
36 The evidence for the disagreement is the baptismal ritual outlined in the *Constitutiones Apostolicae*, a non-Nicene church order credited by fiction to the apostles; its origin is debated, but probably Eunomian (Vaggione, *Eunomius*, 259–60, 339–42, cf. p. 149, n. 20). For an alternative view and much relevant theological background, see Rowan Williams, "Baptism and the Arian Controversy," in *Arianism After Arius: Essays on the Development of the Fourth Century Trinitarian Conflicts*, ed. Michel R. Barnes and Daniel H. Williams (Edinburgh: T&T Clark, 1993), 149–80.
37 Cf. Vaggione, *Eunomius*, 342.
38 Philostorgius, 10.4.
39 Epiphanius, *Panarion* 76.4.
40 Gregory of Nazianzus, *Oratio* 29.7.
41 Philostorgius, 10.1, 3.
42 Note, however, that a letter, written in the 550s by Pelagius I of Rome (*Epistula* 21), attests to similar practices among "heretics" near Sirmium and Singidunum in the Balkans. Granted the location, these are most likely Homoians, who would seem then to have followed a similar logic to (or been influenced by) the Eunomians of Constantinople. Marta Szada, *Conversion and the Contest of Creeds in Early Medieval Christianity* (Cambridge: Cambridge University Press, 2024), 130, suggests, however, that they were Eunomians.

## CHAPTER 7: THE TURN TO PNEUMATOLOGY

1 Socrates, 2.45, and Sozomen, 4.27, connect it to Macedonius's deposition from the bishopric of Constantinople by Acacius and Eudoxius in 360.
2 *The Letters of Saint Athanasius Concerning the Holy Spirit*, trans. C.R.B. Shapland (London: Epworth Press, 1951), 23.
3 Barnes, "Beginning and End."
4 McCarthy Spoerl and Vinzent, *Eusebius*, 48–50; Eusebius of Caesarea, *De ecclesiastica theologia* 3.4–6.

5 Eusebius of Caesarea, *De ecclesiastica theologia* 3.5.17–18.
6 Eusebius of Caesarea, *De ecclesiastica theologia* 3.6.1–2.
7 *Letters of Saint Athanasius*, 27
8 Athanasius, *Epistula ad Serapionem* 1.1
9 Athanasius, *Epistula ad Serapionem* 1.1, 10
10 Athanasius, *Epistula ad Serapionem* 1.10.
11 Athanasius, *Epistula ad Serapionem,* 3.1.
12 Athanasius, *Epistula ad Serapionem* 3.5, 7. See Mark DelCogliano, Andrew Radde-Gallwitz, and Lewis Ayres, *Works on the Spirit: Athanasius the Great and Didymus the Blind* (Yonkers, NY: St. Vladimir's Seminary Press, 2011), 17.
13 *Dok.* 62.5 (Athanasius, *De synodis* 30.20–10, Socrates, 2.41.8–16).
14 Eunomius, *Apologia* 25.
15 Eunomius, *Apologia* 25.
16 DelCogliano, Radde-Gallwitz, and Ayres, *Works on the Spirit*, 181 n. 141; Gregory of Nyssa, *Contra Eunomium* 2.33. Basil's response likely belongs in 364 or 365: Vaggione, *Eunomius: The Extant Works*, 5–6.
17 Eunomius, *Expositio fidei* 4.
18 DelCogliano *et al.*, *Works on the Spirit*, 40.
19 Socrates, 2.42–43; Philostorgius, 5.1.
20 Socrates, 2.44–45.
21 Sozomen, 4.27.
22 Socrates, 2.45.2–4.
23 Socrates, 4.4, Sozomen, 6.7–8.
24 Socrates, 4.12; Sozomen, 6.11 (including a letter from Eustathius, Theophilus, and Silvanus: *Dok.* 77.5). The delegation need not have set out immediately after the Lampsacus council, but certainly will have reached Rome before Liberius's death in September 366: Brennecke *et al.*, *Dokumente* 4:713–14).
25 *Dok.* 77.6 (Socrates, 4.12.22–37).
26 Hilary, *De synodis* 90.
27 Hilary, *De synodis* 31.
28 For more on this, see Manlio Simonetti, "Note di cristologia pneumatica," *Augustinianum* 12, no. 2 (1972): 201–32; Pierre Smulders, *La doctrine trinitaire de s. Hilaire de Poitiers* (Rome: Universitas Gregoriana, 1944), 235.
29 Basil of Caesarea, *Epistula* 223.5. Some manuscripts of this letter further say that Eustathius and Basil visited with Silvanus at this point. It is excluded from Courtonne's edition but is unlikely to be an interpolation.

See *Saint Basile: Lettres*, ed. and trans. Yves Courtonne, vol. 3, Collection Budé (Paris: Belles Lettres, 1966), 14.

30 Gregory of Nazianzus, *Epistula* 58. See Timothy P. McConnell, *Illumination in Basil of Caesarea's Doctrine of the Holy Spirit* (Minneapolis, MN: Fortress Press, 2017), 2, and Oliver B. Langworthy, *Gregory of Nazianzus' Soteriological Pneumatology*, Studien und Texte zu Antike und Christentum 117 (Tübingen: Mohr Siebeck, 2019), 72–75.

31 Gregory of Nazianzus, *Oratio* 41.7

32 Gregory of Nazianzus, *Oratio* 41.8.

33 Gregory of Nyssa, *Adversus Macedonianos, de Spiritu Sancto*, in Werner Jaeger, *Gregorii Nysseni Opera*, vol. III/1, *Gregorii Nysseni Opera Dogmtica Minora* (Leiden: Brill), 89, at l. 18. Cf. Giulio Maspero, "The Fire, the Kingdom and the Glory: The Creator Spirit and the Intra-Trinitarian Processions in the *Adversus Macedonianos* of Gregory of Nyssa," in *Gregory of Nyssa: The Minor Treatises on Trinitarian Theology and Apollinarianism*, ed. Volker Henning Drecoll and Margitta Berghaus, Supplements to Vigiliae Christianae 106 (Leiden: Brill, 2011), 229–76, at 244.

34 Basil of Caesarea, *De Spiritu Sancto* 13.29.

35 Cf. Barnes, "Beginning and End," 184.

36 DelCogliano *et al.*, *Works on the Holy Spirit*, 14–15.

37 Cf. Michael A.G. Haykin, *The Spirit of God: The Exegesis of 1 and 2 Corinthians in the Pneumatomachian Controversy of the Fourth Century*, Supplements to Vigiliae Christianae (Leiden: Brill, 1994), 181.

38 *Codex Theodosianus* 16.1.2.

39 Background in Henry Chadwick, *The Church in Ancient Society: From Galilee to Gregory the Great* (Oxford: Oxford University Press, 2001), 415–32.

40 "Normative bishops": Adolf Martin Ritter, "Councils and Synods," in *The Brill Dictionary of Gregory of Nyssa*, ed. Lucas Francisco Mateo-Seco and Giulio Maspero, Supplements to Vigiliae Christianae 99 (Boston: Brill, 2010), 180–82, at 181.

41 Gregory of Nazianzus, *De vita sua* 1525–34, describes his apparent belief that he could achieve peace between the Antiochene factions. See Christopher Beeley, *Gregory of Nazianzus on the Trinity and the Knowledge of God: In Your Light We Shall See Light*, Oxford Studies in Historical Theology (Oxford: Oxford University Press, 2008), 46.

42 Socrates, 5.8.5–10.

43 Gregory of Nazianzus, *De vita sua* 1799–800.

44 For the rupture with Nyssen, see Beeley, *Trinity*, 49 n. 165 and John McGuckin, *St. Gregory of Nazianzus: An Intellectual Biography* (Crestwood, NY: St Vladimir's Seminary Press, 2001), 356.
45 *Codex Theodosianus* 16.1.3.
46 *Codex Theodosianus* 16.5.6.
47 The text of the creed of 381 is first encountered in the acts of the council of Chalcedon in 451. Its relationship to the council continues to be discussed, but the creed, preserved in a sermon of Nestorius, that is the main alternative claimant to be the council's final statement (Kinzig, *A History of Early Christian Creeds*, 366), contains substantially the same language about the Holy Spirit.
48 Theodoret, 5.9.
49 Thomas Graumann, "The Synod of Constantinople, AD 383: History and Historiography," *Millenium* 7, no. 1 (2010): 133–68.
50 Socrates, 5.10.24–26.
51 *Codex Theodosianus* 16.5.11.
52 For which, e.g., McLynn, *Ambrose*, 158–219.

## CHAPTER 8: GOTHIC HOMOIANISM

1 On the Danube crossing, Adrianople, and its aftermath, see Ammianus Marcellinus, bk. 31; Peter J. Heather, *Goths and Romans, 332–489*, Oxford Historical Monographs (Oxford: Oxford University Press, 1994).
2 Several members of the Burgundian ruling family, especially women, were Catholics (Uta Heil, *Avitus von Vienne und die homöische Kirche der Burgunder*, Patristische Texte und Studien 66 (Berlin: De Gruyter, 2011), 48–66).
3 The conversion of the (Terving) immigrants of the late 370s is best attested, but reconstruction is uncertain: Peter Heather, "The Crossing of the Danube and the Gothic Conversion," *Greek, Roman and Byzantine Studies* 27, no. 3 (1986): 289–318; Noel Lenski, "The Gothic Civil War and the Date of the Gothic Conversion," *Greek, Roman and Byzantine Studies* 36, no. 1 (1995): 51–87.
4 The date is uncertain; see, e.g., Peter Heather and John Matthews, *The Goths in the Fourth Century*, Translated Texts for Historians 11 (Liverpool: Liverpool University Press, 1991), 132–33.
5 Socrates, 2.41.22–3, Sozomen, 4.24.1.
6 Auxentius of Durostorum, *Epistula* 33; Philostorgius, 2.5.
7 Briefly mentioned at p. 64.

8 The manuscript is catalogued as Paris, Bibliothèque nationale de France, Latinus 8907. The authoritative editions of these marginal notes (*scholia*), both by Roger Gryson, use different numbering systems. We follow *Scripta Arriana Latina I: Collectio Veronensis, Scholia in Concilium Aquileiense, Fragmenta in Lucam rescripta, Fragmenta theologica rescripta*, ed. Roger Gryson, *Corpus Christianorum Series Latina* 87 (Turnhout: Brepols, 1982), 87:149–96 over *Scolies ariennes sur le concile d'Aquilée*, Sources chrétiennes 267 (Paris: Éditions du Cerf, 1980). No English translation exists, except of Auxentius's letter, in Heather and Matthews, *The Goths*, 137–43. For clarity, we will cite Maximinus's introduction as *Dissertatio*, Auxentius's eulogistic letter as *Epistula*, and Palladius's comments as *Scholia*.

9 *Codex Theodosianus* 16.4.1–2.

10 Neil B. McLynn, "From Palladius to Maximinus: Passing the Arian Torch," *Journal of Early Christian Studies* 4, no. 4 (1996): 477–93.

11 Palladius, *Scholia* 94. During the conflict over the Milanese basilicas (p. 87), Ambrose clashed with one Auxentius Mercurinus, possibly this man: see Michael Stuart Williams, *The Politics of Heresy in Ambrose of Milan Community and Consensus in Late Antique Christianity* (Cambridge: Cambridge University Press, 2017), 253–54.

12 Neil B. McLynn, "Little Wolf in the Big City: Ulfila and His Interpreters," in *Wolf Liebeschuetz Reflected: Essays Presented by Colleagues, Friends and Pupils*, ed. John Drinkwater and Benet Salway, Bulletin of the Institute of Classical Studies Supplement 91 (London: Institute of Classical Studies, 2007), 125–35.

13 Sozomen, 6.37.8–9, Socrates, 2.41.23, Theodoret, 4.37.

14 Philostorgius, 2.5.

15 Auxentius, *Epistula* 24–26. The text is often damaged, and some titles may be missing.

16 Auxentius, *Epistula* 27–28.

17 Auxentius, *Epistula* 30.

18 A recent attempt to salvage Wulfila's pneumatology does not convince: Tarmo Toom, "Ulfila's Creedal Statement and Its Theology," *Journal of Early Christian Studies* 29, no. 4 (2021): 525–52, at 547.

19 Auxentius, *Epistula* 40.

20 Most recently, Sara Parvis, "Was Ulfila Really a Homoian?," in *Arianism: Roman Heresy and Barbarian Creed*, ed. Guido M. Berndt and Roland Steinacher (Farnham: Ashgate, 2014), 49–65, with prior scholarship at 49–50 n. 2.

21 Auxentius, *Epistula* 29.

22 See p. 120.

23 Auxentius, *Epistula* 24, directly denies God's comprehensibility; Alain Chauvot, "Ulfila dans l'œuvre de Philostorge," in *Philostorge et l'historiographie de l'Antiquité tardive*, ed. Doris Meyer, with Bruno Bleckmann, Alain Chauvot, and Jean-Marc Prieur, Collegium Beatus Rhenanus 3 (Stuttgart: Franz Steiner, 2011), 289–305.

24 Cf. Volker Menze, "Ariminian Churches in the Germanic Kingdoms," in *Brill Encyclopedia of Early Christianity* (forthcoming).

25 Carla Falluomini, *The Gothic Version of the Gospels and Pauline Epistles: Cultural Background, Transmission and Character*, Arbeiten zur Neutestamentlichen Textforschung 46 (Berlin: De Gruyter, 2015), 35–6, suggests that the lost and very brief, Latin-Gothic *Codex Gissensis* could have been Vandalic, though derived from an Ostrogothic model.

26 All but the Bologna fragments are accessible through the Wulfila Project, www.wulfila.be. For an English translation of the Bologna fragments, see Rosa Bianca Finazzi and Paola Tornaghi, "Gothica bononiensia: A New Document Under Linguistic and Philological Analysis," *Interdisciplinary Journal for Germanic Linguistics and Semiotic Analysis* 19, no. 2 (2014): 1–56.

27 E.g., Socrates, 4.33.7–9.

28 Knut Schäferdiek, "Das gotische liturgische Kalendarfragment—Bruchstück eines Konstantinopeler Martyrologs," repr. in Knut Schäferdiek, *Schwellenzeit: Beiträge zur Geschichte des Christentums in Spätantike und Frühmittelalter*, ed. Winrich A. Löhr and Hanns Christof Brennecke, Arbeiten zur Kirchengeschichte 64 (Berlin: De Gruyter, 1996), 147–68, at 168, suggests translation into Gothic by the Wulfilan community on the Danube.

29 Brendan Wolfe, "The Gothic Palimpsest of Bologna," *Studia Patristica* 92 (2017): 205–8.

30 In technical terms, the Gothic follows a Byzantine text but incorporates "Western" readings: Falluomini, *Gothic Version*, 1.

31 Artūras Ratkus, "Greek ἀρχιερεύς in Gothic Translation: Linguistics and Theology at a Crossroads," *NOWELE* 71, no. 1 (2018): 3–34.

32 Maximinus, in Augustine, *Conlatio cum Maximino* 15.15, as clarified by Augustine, *Contra Maximinum* 1.5.

33 Maximinus's view is anticipated by Athanasius of Anazarbus, radical supporter of Arius and teacher of Aëtius (Bobbio, fragment 4; p. 113).

34 Full discussion and scholarship in Brendan Wolfe and Mattias Gassman, "'A Thing Like God': Re-Reading Gothic Philippians 2.6–8," *New Testament Studies* (forthcoming).
35 Crawford, "Diversity and Influence," Knut Schäferdiek, "Theodor von Herakleia (328/34–351/55): Ein wenig bekannter Kirchenpolitiker und Exeget des vierten Jahrhunderts," repr. in Schäferdiek, *Schwellenzeit*, 51–68.
36 *Skeireins* IVc–d.
37 Aloys Grillmeier, *Christ in Christian Tradition*, vol. 1, *From the Apostolic Age to Chalcedon (451)*, trans. John Bowden, 2nd ed. (London: Mowbray, 1975), 324–26.
38 *Skeireins* IVd, Vb. Cf. Brendan Wolfe, "The Skeireins: a neglected text," *Studia Patristica* 64 (2013): 127–32.
39 *Epistula* 2.9.
40 *De gubernatione dei* 5.5–8.
41 Robin Whelan, *Being Christian in Vandal Africa: The Politics of Orthodoxy in the Post-Imperial West*, The Transformation of the Classical Heritage 59 (Oakland: University of California Press, 2018), 165–94.
42 Ambrose, *De fide* 2.16.140; Maximinus, *Dissertatio* 11; *Opus imperfectum in Matthaeum* (*Patrologia Graeca* 56:626).
43 A point lately reiterated by Marta Szada, "The Missing Link: The Homoian Church in the Danubian Provinces and Its Role in the Conversion of the Goths," *Zeitschrift für Antikes Christentum* 24, no. 3 (2020): 549–84.
44 Hanns Christof Brennecke, "Deconstruction of the So-Called Germanic Arianism," in *Arianism*, ed. Berndt and Steinacher, 117–30.
45 Philostorgius, 2.5.

## CHAPTER 9: LATER HOMOIAN THEOLOGY

1 Along with the letter of Auxentius (p. 91) and the *Sermo Arrianorum*, in *Arianism and Other Heresies*, trans. Roland J. Teske, vol. I/18 of *The Works of St. Augustine* (Hyde Park, NY: New City Press, 1995), 133–40), one of the few Homoian texts available in English translation: *Incomplete Commentary on Matthew (Opus imperfectum)*, trans. James A. Kellerman, ed. Thomas C. Oden, 2 vols., Ancient Christian Texts (Downers Grove, IL: IVP Academic, 2010).
2 The best theological overviews are in French and Italian: Gryson, *Scolies*, 173–200, Simonetti, "Arianesimo latino," 684–744; in English, see

William A. Sumruld, *Augustine and the Arians: The Bishop of Hippo's Encounters with Ulfilan Arianism* (Selinsgrove, PA: Susquehanna University Press, 1994), 46–61. The most comprehensive study, Michel Meslin, *Les Ariens d'occident, 335–430*, Patristica Sorbonensia 8 (Paris: Éditions du Seuil, 1967), is gravely weakened by speculative assignment of specific authors to works transmitted anonymously or pseudonymously.

3 Greek Homoianism survived into the sixth century—Geoffrey Greatrex, "Theodore Lector and the Arians of Constantinople," in *Studies in Theodore Anagnostes*, ed. Rafał Kosiński and Adrian Szopa, Studi e testi tardoantichi 19 (Brepols: Tournhout, 2021), 207–31—but theological information is extremely limited.

4 Pseudo-Fredegarius, *Chronicae* 4.8. A nuanced overview of political and ethnic relations in Whelan, *Being Christian*, 219–50; for fine political detail across the entire West, see Szada, *Conversion and the Contest of Creeds*.

5 Maksim Korobov and Andrey Vinogradov, "Gotische Graffito-Inschriften aus der Bergkrim," *Zeitschrift für deutsches Altertum und deutsche Literatur* 145 (2016); 141–57. A rendering of *Kyrie eleison* ("froia arme") is attested in *Collatio Augustini cum Pascentio* 15, a reimagining of Augustine's dialogue with Count Pascentius (p. 120).

6 Now held at Uppsala University Library in Sweden, https://www.uu.se/en/library/visit-and-contact/exhibitions/codex-argenteus, accessed October 16, 2024.

7 Relayed by Jordanes's *Getica* (on which, Heather, *Goths and Romans*, 3–67).

8 Bryan Ward-Perkins, "Where is the Archaeology and Iconography of Germanic Arianism?," in *Religious Diversity in Late Antiquity*, ed. David M. Gwynn and Susanne Bangert, Late Antique Archaeology 6 (Leiden: Brill, 2010), 265–89, at 281–82.

9 Augustine, *Confessiones* 9.7.15, Socrates, 6.8.1–9, Sozomen, 8.8.

10 Raymond Étaix, "Sermons ariens inédits," *Recherches augustiniennes et patristiques* 26 (1992): 143–79.

11 Roger Gryson, "Les sermons ariens du *Codex latinus monacensis 6329*: Étude critique," *Revue des Études Augustiniennes* 39, no. 2 (1993): 333–58.

12 Étaix, *Sermon* 7.1, 8.

13 Étaix, *Sermon* 9.1, 7.2.

14 Étaix, *Sermon* 7.2, 13.1–2.

15 Étaix, *Sermon* 7.1.

16 Étaix, *Sermon* 7.1, 22.2.

17 Étaix, *Sermon* 12.2.
18 Étaix, *Sermon* 19.
19 Verona, Biblioteca Capitolare, LI (49). Its contents have been edited, with extreme fidelity to the manuscript text, by Roger Gryson, in *Corpus Christianorum Series Latina* 87:3–145.
20 Background in Dieter Hagedorn, *Der Hiobkommenter des Arianers Julian*, Patristische Texte und Studien 14 (Berlin: De Gruyter, 1973), xli–lvii; cf. p. 141, n. 36.
21 Not necessarily read together, however. The palimpsest also includes classical works: Roger Gryson, *Les palimpsestes ariens latins de Bobbio: Contribution à la méthodologie de l'étude des palimpsestes*, Armarium Codicum Insignium 2 (Turnhout: Brepols, 1983). Roger Gryson has edited the fragments of the catechesis and anti-Nicene polemic from Bobbio at *Corpus Christianorum Series Latina* 87:229–65.
22 *Patrologia Graeca* 56:626, 758, 864. In the last passage, the commentator also holds that a military career leads the soldier to hell: a view surely setting him at odds with the "barbarian" Homoians in Roman service.
23 Jerome: Pierre Nautin, "L''Opus imperfectum in Mattheum' et les Ariens de Constantinople," *Revue d'histoire ecclésiastique* 67, no. 2 (1972): 381–408, at 396–99. Apocrypha: *Patrologia Graeca* 56:637–38 (magi), 770, 906, 909, 925 (pseudo-Clementines).
24 Leslie Dossey, "The Last Days of Vandal Africa: An Arian Commentary on Job and Its Historical Context," *Journal of Theological Studies*, n.s., 54, no. 1 (2003): 60–138.
25 *Corpus Christianorum Series Latina* 87:205.
26 *Sermo Arrianorum* 27, 32; Auxentius, *Epistula* 27–28, Palladius, *Scholia* 54, 90–91.
27 Bobbio fragments 7, 8.
28 *Conlatio cum Maximino* 15.15.
29 Note, however, *Patrologia Graeca* 56:820, 886, 889 (denials of pro-Nicene doctrine), 859, and 874.
30 *Conlatio cum Maximino* 15.5, 9, 14–15, 22, *Sermo Arrianorum* 27, Bobbio fragments 17, 22; Étaix, *Sermon* 8 (with Gryson, "Les sermons ariens," 335); Verona Sermons, *De sollemnitatibus* 7.5, 8.2, 12.3; commentary on Luke 1:2, 34 (*Corpus Christianorum Series Latina* 87:200, 206).
31 *Conlatio cum Maximino* 15.9, 13.
32 For example, in Augustine's dispute with Pascentius: Augustine, *Epistula* 238.4–5.
33 Augustine, *Epistula* 238.25, Heil, *Avitus*, 214–20.

34 See still R.P.C. Hanson, "The Arian Doctrine of the Incarnation," in *Arianism: Historical and Theological Reassessments, Papers from The Ninth International Conference on Patristic Studies, September 5–10, 1983, Oxford, England*, ed. Robert C. Gregg, Patristic Monograph Series 11 (Philadelphia: Philadelphia Patristic Foundation, 1985), 181–211.
35 Bobbio fragment 20; Étaix, *Sermon* 7.1.
36 *Conlatio cum Maximino* 12, 15.9.
37 *Patrologia Graeca* 56:653, 658, 777, 788, 853, 859, 889, 919; 825.
38 *Sermo de sollemnitatibus* 7.5.
39 Bobbio fragment 23.
40 *Patrologia Graeca* 56:740, 886.
41 Fastiodosus's discourse is printed at *Corpus Christianorum Series Latina* 91:280–83.
42 *In Iob commentarius* 1.75.
43 *Sermo Arrianorum* 13–19; *Sermo de sollemnitatibus* 7.5.
44 Bobbio fragment 5.
45 *Sermo Arrianorum* 10.
46 *Dok.* 119.4 (Gregory of Tours, *Historia Francorum* 6.18).
47 Edward Siecienski, *The Filioque: History of a Doctrinal Controversy* (Oxford: Oxford University Press, 2010), 68–69.
48 Maurice Wiles, *Archetypal Heresy: Arianism through the Centuries* (Oxford: Oxford University Press, 1996), 50; E.A. Thompson, *The Visigoths in the Time of Ulfila* (Oxford: Clarendon Press, 1966), 123; Sumruld, *Augustine and the Arians*, 57–61.
49 Étaix, *Sermon* 13.2.
50 Étaix, *Sermon* 7.2, 10.2, 14.
51 No English translation exists; for an attempt to tease out one knotty example of his reasoning, see Mattias Gassman, "An Ancient Account of Pagan Origins: Making Sense of Filastrius, *Diuersarum hereseon liber* 111," *Revue d'études augustiniennes et patristiques* 67, no. 1 (2021): 83–105.
52 Pelagian echoes appear in the Job and Matthew commentators: Dossey, "Last Days," 87–89; Fredric W. Schlatter, "The Pelagianism of the Opus Imperfectum in Matthaeum," *Vigiliae Christianae* 41, no. 3 (1987): 267–84. Fastiodosus, by contrast, retained his belief in original sin, after converting to Homoianism. Szada, *Conversion*, 126–27, notes some more examples.
53 Not, however, by mere *linguistic* separation, despite Sumruld, *Augustine and the Arians*, 58–59. Cf. p. 97.

## CHAPTER 10: EUNOMIANS, "ARIANS," AND CHURCH HISTORY

1 Philostorgius, 9.9, 10.6.

2 Relatively few fragments can be confidently ascribed to the "anonymous Arian": Peter Van Nuffelen, "Considérations sur l'anonyme homéen," in *Les historiens fragmentaires de la langue grecque à l'époque romaine impériale et tardive*, ed. Eugenio Amato, Pasqua De Cicco, Bertrand Lançon, and Tiphaine Moreau (Rennes: Presses Universitaires de Rennes, 2021), 207–22. They shed little light on the controversy's evolution.

3 Thomas C. Ferguson, *The Past is Prologue: The Revolution of Nicene Historiography*, Supplements to Vigiliae Christianae 75 (Leiden: Brill, 2005), 125–63, surveys Philostorgius's methods and preoccupations.

4 Philostorgius, 3.5–11; 1.1; 12.8–10, with Peter Van Nuffelen, "Isolement et apocalypse: Philostorge et les eunomiens sous Théodose II," in *Philostorge et l'historiographie de l'Antiquité tardive*, ed. Doris Meyer, with Bruno Bleckmann, Alain Chauvot, and Jean-Marc Prieur, Collegium Beatus Rhenanus 3 (Stuttgart: Franz Steiner, 2011), 307–28.

5 Philostorgius, 1.9, 2.1.

6 Philostorgius, 4.9, 8.17.

7 Philostorgius, 4.11.

8 Annick Martin, "Athanase et les néo-ariens," in Meyer, *Philostorge*, 275–88.

9 Philostorgius, 2.3.

10 Philostorgius, 2.14–15.

11 As indeed, he does throughout the tradition: Hanns Christof Brennecke, "Lukian von Antiochien in der Geschichte des Arianischen Streites," in *Logos: Festschrift für Luise Abramowski zum 8. Juli 1993*, ed. Hanns Christof Brennecke, Ernst Ludwig Grasmück, and Christoph Markschies, Beihefte zur Zeitschrift für die neutestamentliche Wissenschaft 67 (Berlin: De Gruyter, 1993), 170–92.

12 Philostorgius, 3.15, 17. Letter: chap. 3, above.

13 Introduced at Philostorgius, 2.6.

14 Introduced at Philostorgius, 3.16.

15 Thus a separate, much briefer summary, in Photius, *Bibliotheca*, codex 40, 8b.

16 Philostorgius, 5.1, 6.4.

17 This speech is not the extant *Apologia*: Vaggione, *Eunomius: The Extant Works*, 6–7.

18 Philostorgius, 6.1–3.

19 Philostorgius, 7.5–6.
20 Philostorgius, 8.2–4, 9.3.
21 Philostorgius, 9.13; cf. 6.1.
22 Philostorgius, 9.14, 14a (an entry on Demophilus in the Byzantine encyclopedia, the *Souda*).
23 Philostorgius, 10.2–3; Kopecek, *History*, 512.
24 Philostorgius, 3.19, on Secundus of Ptolemais, exiled—as Philostorgius, 1.9–10, acknowledges—with Arius and Theonas of Marmarica.
25 See pp. 90–91.
26 Bobbio fragments 1–12 (*Corpus Christianorum Series Latina* 87:229–47).
27 Palladius, *Scholia* 83.
28 Maximinus, *Dissertatio* 11.
29 Palladius, *Scholia* 61, 64, 66.
30 Maximinus, *Dissertatio* 22.
31 The argument ultimately builds toward a complex—and erroneous—reconstruction of the motivations behind Theodosius's Council of the Sects in 383: McLynn, "From Palladius to Maximinus."
32 Phoebadius: Sulpicius Severus, *Chronica* 2.44.6–8.
33 Bobbio fragment 3; Palladius, *Scholia* 83.
34 Bobbio fragment 4; *Urk.* 11 (Athanasius, *De synodis* 17.4), with Hanson, "Who Taught ἐξ οὐκ ὄντων?"
35 *In Iob commentarius* 2.31.
36 *Conlatio cum Maximino* 2.
37 For the list, apart from Wulfila, Palladius, *Scholia* 94.
38 Cf. *Corpus Christianorum Series Latina* 87:xxv.
39 One doubts he was the Arian Maximinus (Hydatius, *Chronicon* 120) who betrayed Palermo, Sicily, to the Vandals in 440 (so, e.g., R.W. Mathisen, "Sigisvult the Patrician, Maximinus the Arian, and Political Strategems in the Western Roman Empire, *c.* 425–40," *Early Medieval Europe* 8, no. 2 (1999): 173–96, at 185–87).
40 *Conlatio cum Maximino* 13.
41 *Conlatio cum Maximino* 15.9.
42 Philostorgius, 4.12, 5.1, 6.3, 7.6.
43 Philostorgius, 9.8.
44 Philostorgius, 2.5.
45 Socrates, 5.23, 24.1–6, Sozomen, 6.26.1–10, 7.17; Philostorgius, 12.11.
46 Likewise, Theodoret, 4.37.4, reports that "the Goths" would not call the Son a "created being," a term ascribed to Christ by the Eunomian confession preserved as Eunomius, *Apologia* 28; the "Exposition of Patricius and Aëtius," *Dok.* 75.1 (*Historia Acephala* 4.6), even affirms the Son's existence *ex nihilo*.

47 Philostorgius, 2.15.
48 *Epistula* 238.4.
49 *Patrologia Graeca* 56: 635.
50 Philostorgius, 6.2.
51 The Goth Fl. Plinta, consul 419, effected an agreement, but the schism endured elsewhere: Socrates, 5.23.12.
52 Philostorgius, 12.11.
53 *Novella* 3.9 of Theodosius II, adopted into the law code ("Breviary") of Alaric II: Gustav Hänel, *Lex Romana Visigothorum* (Berlin: Wilhelm Besser, 1849), 258.

## CONCLUSION

1 Thus (referencing "hair-splitters") as early as Charles Darwin, Letter to J.D. Hooker, August 1, [1875], Letter no. 2130, Darwin Correspondence Project, https://www.darwinproject.ac.uk/letter/?docId=letters/DCP-LETT-2130.xml, accessed October 16, 2024.
2 A term cited in Augustine, *Contra Iulianum opus imperfectum* 1.75 (an unfinished anti-Pelagian work, not to be confused with the Homoian *Opus imperfectum in Matthaeum* falsely attributed to John Chrysostom).
3 Here Kinzig, *A History of Early Christian Creeds*, is fundamental.

# FURTHER READING

## GENERAL SURVEYS AND COLLECTIONS

Hanson, R.P.C. *The Search for the Christian Doctrine of God: The Arian Controversy, 318–381*. Edinburgh: T&T Clark, 1988.

A comprehensive account of Christian thinking on the nature of God, from the outbreak of the Arian controversy to the Council of Constantinople 381. Relatively thin on late Eunomianism and Homoianism—though much can be gleaned by an attentive reader—and tends to posit a theologically coherent "Arianism" stretching, amid genuine variation, from Arius and his allies to writers active after 381. Explicitly or implicitly underlies many later studies. Indispensable and vast.

Simonetti, Manlio. *La crisi ariana nel IV secolo*. Studia Ephemeridis "Augustinianum" 11. Rome: Institutum Patristicum "Augustinianum," 1975.

The Italian counterpart to Hanson's study, by a pre-eminent twentieth-century Patristic scholar (and a defender of the concept of "Arianism"). For Latin non-Nicenism after the 380s, consult his "Arianesimo latino," *Studi medievali*, 3rd s., 8 (1967): 663–744, which interprets the later Homoians as theologically Eunomian.

Lewis, Ayres. *Nicaea and Its Legacy: An Approach to Fourth-Century Trinitarian Theology*. Oxford: Oxford University Press, 2004.

The standard account reflecting key developments in scholarship after Hanson's and Simonetti's surveys (especially suspicion over the utility of "Arianism" as a concept). First two parts narrate the formation of the pro-Nicene consensus, amid alternatives. The narrative consciously ends before the further development of that consensus in the West (described in *Augustine and the Trinity*, Cambridge: Cambridge University Press, 2010). Concluding section explores the relevance of ancient pro-Nicene thought to modern Trinitarian theology.

Wiles, Maurice. *Archetypal Heresy: Arianism through the Centuries*. Oxford: Oxford University Press, 1996.

A brief survey of "Arianism" ranging beyond the ancient controversy to its later reception. Of particular historical interest is the lengthy chapter 5, on the early modern British "Arians" (Isaac Newton the most famous) and the demise of their theology in favor of Unitarianism and deism.

Anatolios, Khaled. *Retrieving Nicaea: The Development and Meaning of Trinitarian Doctrine*. Foreword by Brian E. Daley. Grand Rapids, MI: Baker Academic, 2011.

A focused but extremely clear account of the development of Nicene Trinitarian theology in the works of Athanasius of Alexandria, Gregory of Nyssa, and Augustine of Hippo. Fundamentally a theological and not a historical treatment; but in so orienting itself, it provides a ready entry point into three foundational thinkers. The treatment of Athanasius is especially valuable.

Kim, Young Richard, ed. *The Cambridge Companion to the Council of Nicaea*. Cambridge: Cambridge University Press, 2021.

Sixteen up-to-date articles on the context, events, theological results, and later reception of Nicaea 325. Note especially chapters 7–9, which discuss the wider theological and disciplinary effects of the council (including its creed, canons, and impact on Easter celebrations) and 11–14, which offer a succinct overview of important later developments in (mostly) pro-Nicene theology.

Kelly, J.N.D. *Early Christian Creeds*. 3rd ed. London: Longman, 1972.

For decades, the standard account of the formation and proliferation of creedal statements in the ancient church. Still the most approachable survey for the general reader. An up-to-date (and at times necessarily quite complicated) account is offered by Wolfram Kinzig, *A History of Early Christian Creeds* (Berlin: De Gruyter, 2024), which synthesizes the massive body of evidence presented in his four-volume *Faith in Formulae: A Collection of Early Christian Creeds and Creed-related Texts*. Oxford Early Christian Texts (Oxford: Oxford University Press, 2017).

## PART I

Williams, Rowan. *Arius: Heresy and Tradition*. Rev. ed. Grand Rapids, MI: Eerdmans, 2001.

A dense but illuminating study of what can reliably be said, and what might reasonably be guessed, about Arius's thinking and its theological underpinnings. Includes close discussion of predecessors Jewish (Philo), Christian (Clement of Alexandria, Origen), and pagan (especially the Neoplatonist Plotinus). First published in 1987; appendix to revised edition surveys scholarship in the interim.

Gregg, Robert C., and Dennis E. Groh. *Early Arianism: A View of Salvation*. Philadelphia: Fortress Press, 1981.

A speculative account of the theological motivations underlying the view of the deity advanced by Arius and his allies. Infers, from the polemics of Alexander and Athanasius, that "Arianism" was inspired by an adoptionist soteriology: the only-begotten Son, being perfected in view of his future virtues, is a model for what we may also become.

Gwynn, David M. *The Eusebians: The Polemic of Athanasius of Alexandria and the Construction of the "Arian Controversy."* Oxford Theological Monographs. Oxford: Oxford University Press, 2007.

The methodological antithesis to Gregg and Groh: a consistently skeptical deconstruction of Athanasius's representation of his opponents. Includes valuable discussion of the dating of his works and of the fine details of the thinking of various "Eusebian" churchmen. Tends to assume that ideas unattested in the (very limited) surviving documents penned by Arius and his allies were invented by way of polemic.

Johnson, Aaron P. *Eusebius*. Understanding Classics. London: Bloomsbury. 2013.

A helpful entry point into the thought of Eusebius of Caesarea, in theological and historical context. Alongside a very complete accounting of the works of Eusebius it elucidates the political dynamics which shaped his thought.

Renberg, Adam. *The Son is Truly Son: The Trinitarian and Christological Theology of Eusebius of Caesarea*. Studia Traditionis Theologiae 46. Turnhout: Brepols, 2021.

A necessary volume for anyone wishing to delve more deeply into the theology of Eusebius of Caesarea. Coverage is extensive, extending into Eusebius's canon tables. Particularly valuable for its highlighting of the theological stakes of Eusebius's historical moment and for revealing the exegetical bases of Eusebius's Trinitarian theology.

Cartwright, Sophie. *The Theological Anthropology of Eustathius of Antioch*. Oxford Early Christian Studies. Oxford: Oxford University Press, 2015.

An account of the anthropological and Christological ideas of a neglected pro-Nicene preserved largely in fragments. Helps to flesh out early Nicene thought ordinarily dominated by Alexander, Athanasius, and Marcellus, and so by Trinitarian concerns.

Lienhard, Joseph T. *Contra Marcellum: Marcellus of Ancyra and Fourth-Century Theology*. Washington, DC: Catholic University of America Press, 1999.

A succinct guide to the thinking of the great bugbear of non-Nicene churchmen down to ca. 350, and to ongoing polemic against his ideas, among pro-Nicenes, over the following decades. Includes valuable discussion both of the "two-hypostases" theology that Marcellus opposed and of particular exponents including Asterius and Eusebius of Caesarea.

Parvis, Sara. *Marcellus of Ancyra and the Lost Years of the Arian Controversy 325–345*. Oxford Early Christian Studies. Oxford: Oxford University Press, 2006.

A serious and thoughtful treatment of Marcellus of Ancyra, which reconsiders the traditional narrative of the council of Nicaea. An essential, though sometimes speculative, study on an overlooked figure in Trinitarian theology—tending toward his rehabilitation as a theological thinker—and of the events down to the 340s.

## PART II

Brennecke, Hanns Christof. *Studien zur Geschichte der Homöer: Der Osten bis zum Ende der homöischen Reichskirche*. Beiträge zur historischen Theologie 73. Tübingen: J.C.B. Mohr (Paul Siebeck), 1988.

The authoritative study of Homoian churchmanship in the East, down to the death of the emperor Valens. Opening chapters present a vision of early Homoianism, highly influential on German scholarship, as a theological current opposed simultaneously to Arius and to Marcellus.

Vaggione, Richard Paul. *Eunomius of Cyzicus and the Nicene Revolution*. Oxford Early Christian Studies. Oxford: Oxford University Press, 2000.

A colossally learned study of the roots, theological significance, and historical trajectory of the most radical branch of non-Nicene thought after Arius himself. Footnotes are a goldmine of primary sources. Tends to assimilate the later, Western Homoians to the Eunomians. Narrative focuses on Aëtius's and Eunomius's own day, but is indebted, in its deep structures, to Philostorgius's fifth-century Eunomian history.

Barnes, Timothy D. *Athanasius and Constantius: Theology and Politics in the Constantinian Empire.* Cambridge, MA: Harvard University Press, 1993.

An exacting narrative of the church politics of the mid-fourth century, beginning before the death of Constantine (337) and extending after the death of Constantius II (361), in tandem with a close, sometimes jaundiced consideration of Athanasius's rhetoric across his corpus.

Barnes, Michel R., and Daniel H. Williams, eds. *Arianism after Arius: Essays on the Development of the Fourth Century Trinitarian Conflicts.* Edinburgh: T&T Clark, 1993.

A collection covering key aspects of the Arian controversy after Arius's own lifetime. Articles on Arius's role (purely rhetorical, with little serious theological consideration) in later polemics (Maurice Wiles), on the Homoiousians (Winrich Löhr), and on baptismal practice and its Trinitarian aspects (Rowan Williams) are especially valuable.

## PART III

Williams, Daniel H. *Ambrose of Milan and the End of the Arian-Nicene Conflicts.* Oxford Early Christian Studies. Oxford: Clarendon Press, 1995.

A study of the imperially sponsored Homoian church in the West, from Rimini 359 to the 380s, and of the rise of a pro-Nicene alternative through the efforts of Hilary and others, especially Ambrose. Includes useful discussions of particular, often neglected churchmen such as Zeno of Verona, to be supplemented by the author's superb "Another Exception to Later Fourth-Century 'Arian' Typologies: The Case of Germinius of Sirmium," *Journal of Early Christian Studies* 4, no. 3 (1996): 335–57.

McLynn, Neil B. *Ambrose of Milan: Church and Court in a Christian Capital.* The Transformation of the Classical Heritage 22. Berkeley: University of California Press, 1994.

A revision, now generally accepted, to older, more triumphalist narratives of Ambrose's relationship to the courts of Gratian, Valentinian II, and

Theodosius I. Presents Ambrose as an adroit politician, carefully managing his public image and maneuvering through the uncertainties of imperial power.

Heather, Peter, and John Matthews. *The Goths in the Fourth Century*. Translated Texts for Historians 11. Liverpool: Liverpool University Press, 1991.

A particularly useful English-language resource on Wulfila, his career, and early Gothic Christianity in general. Includes introductory materials and notes, along with translations of the letter of Auxentius, other ancient materials on Wulfila, an account of a Gothic martyr (Sabas), and other texts, as well as archeological information.

Thompson, E.A. *The Visigoths in the Time of Ulfila*. Oxford: Clarendon Press, 1966.

Though superseded at many points, still the foundational English-language study of fourth-century Gothic culture, including Homoian Christianity.

Schäferdiek, Knut. *Schwellenzeit: Beiträge zur Geschichte des Christentums in Spätantike und Frühmittelalter*. Edited by Winrich A. Löhr and Hanns Christof Brennecke. Arbeiten zur Kirchengeschichte 64. Berlin: De Gruyter, 1996.

Articles by a leading historian of Gothic Christianity. Includes studies of Wulfila, the Greek antecessor of the *Skeireins* (Theodore of Heraclea), and the Gothic church calendar.

Falluomini, Carla. *The Gothic Version of the Gospels and Pauline Epistles: Cultural Background, Transmission and Character*. Arbeiten zur Neutestamentlichen Textforschung 46. Berlin: De Gruyter, 2015.

An up-to-date view on the Gothic Bible, focused especially on Matthew, John, Romans, and Galatians. Includes description of all known Gothic New Testament manuscripts.

## PART IV

Ferguson, Thomas C. *The Past is Prologue: The Revolution of Nicene Historiography*. Supplements to Vigiliae Christianae 75 (Leiden: Brill, 2005).

The fifth chapter analyzes Philostorgius's methods and preoccupations, placing him in the context of contemporary, fifth-century pro-Nicene historiography.

Meyer, Doris, ed., with Bruno Bleckmann, Alain Chauvot, and Jean-Marc Prieur. *Philostorge et l'historiographie de l'Antiquité tardive*. Collegium Beatus Rhenanus 3. Stuttgart: Franz Steiner, 2011.

A wide-ranging collection on Philostorgius. Most studies focus on his sources or relationship to secular historians; note especially the chapters on his and Sozomen's account of the councils of 359 (Guy Sabbah), Philostorgius's depiction of Wulfila (Alain Chauvot), the parallels between his methods and Athanasius's (Annick Martin), and the relationship between the apocalyptic themes of his history and his church's embattled position (Peter Van Nuffelen).

Gryson, Roger, ed. *Scolies ariennes sur le concile d'Aquilée: Introduction, texte latin, traduction et notes*. Sources chrétiennes 267. Paris: Éditions du Cerf, 1980.

Text, with French translation, of the works by Maximinus (including the letter of Auxentius of Durostorum) and Palladius of Ratiaria rebutting Ambrose's actions at Aquileia in 381. Includes the official acts of the council and detailed analysis of Homoian theology. Together with the wider edition of Latin Homoian materials in *Corpus Christianorum Series Latina* 87 (Turnhout: Brepols, 1982), a model of text-critical scholarship. Like Manlio Simonetti, sees the Homoians as in fact Eunomian.

Meslin, Michel. *Les Ariens d'occident, 335–430*. Patristica Sorbonensia 8. Paris: Éditions du Seuil, 1967.

Still the most comprehensive account of non-Nicene churchmen and theology in the West, from the beginning at the synod of Tyre in 335 to the *Opus Imperfectum in Matthaeum* and other late works. Posits a hardening of Homoian Christianity from a moderate initial position to strong subordinationism ca. 380. Much too speculative about authorship of many works.

Sumruld, William A. *Augustine and the Arians: The Bishop of Hippo's Encounters with Ulfilan Arianism*. Selinsgrove, PA: Susquehanna University Press, 1994.

A study of Augustine's anti-Arian works, including his encounter with Maximinus in 427. Includes a brief and readable account of Homoian theology and exegesis. Too negative about Homoian "biblicism."

McLynn, Neil B. "The 'Apology' of Palladius: Nature and Purpose." *Journal of Theological Studies*, n.s., 42, no. 1 (1991): 52–76; "From Palladius to Maximinus: Passing the Arian Torch." *Journal of Early Christian Studies* 4, no. 4 (1996): 477–93; "Little Wolf in the Big City: Ulfila and His Interpreters." In *Wolf Liebeschuetz Reflected: Essays Presented by Colleagues, Friends and Pupils*. Edited by John Drinkwater and Benet Salway. Bulletin of the Institute of Classical Studies Supplement 91, 125–35. London: Institute of Classical Studies, 2007.

Three studies that move well beyond Sumruld and Meslin.

Berndt, Guido M., and Roland Steinacher, eds. *Arianism: Roman Heresy and Barbarian Creed*. Farnham: Ashgate, 2014.

Together with McLynn's articles, the best English-language scholarship on the later Homoians. Particularly valuable for competing views on the relevance (Hanns Christof Brennecke) or inapplicability (Sara Parvis) of the classification "Homoian," a survey of Homoian thinking down to Augustine's day (Uta Heil), demolition of the idea of a distinctive "Germanic" Arianism (Brennecke), and studies of Homoian activity across various regions of the West.

# WORKS CITED

## PRIMARY TEXTS

In addition to the series of *Urkunden* and *Dokumente* listed under the initial "Note on Sources," we have sought to use the latest modern editions of the relevant ancient texts. Most of these are published in series such as *Die griechischen christlichen Schriftsteller der ersten Jahrhunderte* (for Epiphanius, Eusebius, and the other church historians); *Corpus Christianorum, Series Latina* (especially important for the Latin Arian texts); *Corpus Scriptorum Ecclesiasticorum Latinorum* (likewise for Latin material, including Sulpicius Severus, the Arian Job commentary, and Hilary's anti-Arian collection); *Sources chrétiennes* and Budé/Collections des universités de France (for authors including Basil); as well as in series or individual publications dedicated to individual authors, such as *Athanasius Werke*.

Readers without access to specialist libraries will be able to find early modern editions of many of the relevant works in the standard nineteenth-century collections, Jacques-Paul Migne's *Patrologia Latina* and *Patrologia Graeca*. In some cases, as with the *Opus imperfectum in Matthaeum*, the old texts reprinted by Migne are still the standard due to the absence of more recent editions. Critical modern editions have sometimes also entered the public domain, as is the case with early volumes of the *Corpus Scriptorum Ecclesiasticorum Latinorum* and of *Die griechischen christlichen Schriftsteller der ersten Jahrhunderte*, in particular. Besides the public-domain Nicene and Post-Nicene Fathers series, which offers a broad but incomplete sampling of Patristic texts, and the other translations discussed in the "Note on Sources" that follows our introduction, English translations are often available in series such as the Fathers of the Church, published by the Catholic University of America Press, or Ancient Christian Writers, published by Paulist Press.

## MODERN STUDIES


Anatolios, Khaled. *Retrieving Nicaea: The Development and Meaning of Trinitarian Doctrine*. Foreword by Brian E. Daley. Grand Rapids, MI: Baker Academic, 2011.

Ayres, Lewis. *Nicaea and Its Legacy: An Approach to Fourth-Century Trinitarian Theology*. Oxford: Oxford University Press, 2004.

Barnes, Michel René. *Augustine and Nicene Theology: Essays on Augustine and the Latin Argument for Nicaea*. Eugene, OR: Cascade Books, 2023.

———. "The Beginning and End of Early Christian Pneumatology." *Augustinian Studies* 39, no. 2 (2008): 169–86.

Barnes, Michel R., and Daniel H. Williams, eds. *Arianism after Arius: Essays on the Development of the Fourth Century Trinitarian Conflicts*. Edinburgh: T&T Clark, 1993.

Barnes, Timothy D. *Athanasius and Constantius: Theology and Politics in the Constantinian Empire*. Cambridge, MA: Harvard University Press, 1993.

———. *Constantine and Eusebius*. Cambridge, MA: Harvard University Press, 1981.

———. Review of *Eusebians* by David Gwynn, *Journal of Theological Studies* 58, no. 2 (2007): 715–18.

Beckwith, Carl. *Hilary of Poitiers on the Trinity: From De Fide to De Trinitate*. Oxford Early Christian Studies. Oxford: Oxford University Press, 2008.

Beeley, Christopher. *Gregory of Nazianzus on the Trinity and the Knowledge of God: In Your Light We Shall See Light*. Oxford Studies in Historical Theology. Oxford: Oxford University Press, 2008.

Berndt, Guido M., and Roland Steinacher, eds. *Arianism: Roman Heresy and Barbarian Creed*. Farnham: Ashgate, 2014.

Brennecke, Hanns Christof. "'Apollinaristischer Arianismus' oder 'arianischer Apollinarismus': Ein dogmengeschichtliches Konstrukt? Arianische Christologie und Apollinarius von Laodicea." In *Apollinarius und seine Folgen*, edited by Silke-Petra Bergjan, Benjamin J. Gleede, and Martin Heimgartner, 73–92. Studien und Texte zu Antike und Christentum 79. Tübingen: Mohr Siebeck, 2015.

———. "Deconstruction of the So-Called Germanic Arianism." In Berndt and Steinacher, eds., *Arianism*, 117–30.

———. "Homöismus und Logostheologie." In *Logos der Vernunft—Logos des Glaubens*, edited by Ferdinand R. Prostmeier and Horacio E. Lona, 323–38. Berlin: De Gruyter, 2010.

———. "Lukian von Antiochien in der Geschichte des Arianischen Streites." In *Logos: Festschrift für Luise Abramowski zum 8. Juli 1993*, edited by

Hanns Christof Brennecke, Ernst Ludwig Grasmück, and Christoph Markschies, 170–92. Beihefte zur Zeitschrift für die neutestamentliche Wissenschaft 67. Berlin: De Gruyter, 1993.

———. *Studien zur Geschichte der Homöer: Der Osten bis zum Ende der homöischen Reichskirche.* Beiträge zur historischen Theologie 73. Tübingen: J.C.B. Mohr (Paul Siebeck), 1988.

Cartwright, Sophie. *The Theological Anthropology of Eustathius of Antioch.* Oxford Early Christian Studies. Oxford: Oxford University Press, 2015.

Chadwick, Henry. *The Church in Ancient Society: From Galilee to Gregory the Great.* Oxford: Oxford University Press, 2001.

Chauvot, Alain. "Ulfila dans l'œuvre de Philostorge." In Meyer, ed., *Philostorge*, 289–305.

Colish, Marcia L. *The Stoic Tradition from Antiquity to the Early Middle Ages*, vol. 2, *Stoicism in Christian Latin Thought through the Sixth Century*, 2nd ed. Studies in the History of Christian Thought 35. Leiden: Brill, 1990.

Crawford, Matthew R. "On the Diversity and Influence of the Eusebian Alliance: The Case of Theodore of Heraclea." *Journal of Ecclesiastical History* 64, no. 2 (2013): 227–57.

DelCogliano, Mark. "Eusebian Theologies of the Son as the Image of God before 341." *Journal of Early Christian Studies* 14, no. 4 (2006): 459–84.

———. "George of Laodicea: A Historical Reassessment." *Journal of Ecclesiastical History* 62, no. 4 (2011): 667–92.

———. "How Did Arius Learn from Asterius? On the Relationship between the Thalia and the Syntagmation." *Journal of Ecclesiastical History* 69, no. 3 (2018): 477–92.

DelCogliano, Mark, Andrew Radde-Gallwitz, and Lewis Ayres, *Works on the Spirit: Athanasius the Great and Didymus the Blind.* Yonkers, NY: St. Vladimir's Seminary Press, 2011.

di Berardino, Angelo. *Patrology*, vol. 4. Westminster, Maryland: Christian Classics, 1986.

Dossey, Leslie. "The Last Days of Vandal Africa: An Arian Commentary on Job and Its Historical Context." *Journal of Theological Studies,* n.s., 54, no. 1 (2003): 60–138.

Duval, Yves-Marie. "La 'manœuvre frauduleuse' de Rimini: À la recherche du *Liber aduersus Vrsacium et Valentum.*" Chap. 2 in *L'Extirpation de l'Arianisme en Italie du Nord et en Occident. Rimini (359/60) et Aquilée (381), Hilaire de Poitiers (†367/8) et Ambroise de Milan (†397).* Aldershot: Ashgate, 1998. Originally published in *Hilaire et son temps Actes du colloque de Poitiers (29 septembre–3 octobre 1968) à l'occasion du XVIe centenaire de la mort de saint Hilaire* (Paris: Études Augustiniennes, 1969), 51–103.

Edwards, Mark. "Is Subordinationism a Heresy?" *TheoLogica: An International Journal for Philosophy of Religion and Philosophical Theology* 4, no. 2 (2020): 69–86.

———. *Origen Against Plato*. Ashgate Studies in Philosophy and Theology in Late Antiquity. Aldershot: Ashgate, 2002.

*Epitome of the Ecclesiastical History of Philostorgius, compiled by Photius, Patriarch of Constantinople*. Translated by Edward Walford. London: Henry G. Bohn, 1855.

Étaix, Raymond. "Sermons ariens inédits." *Recherches augustiniennes et patristiques* 26 (1992): 143–79.

*Eusebius of Caesarea, Against Marcellus and On Ecclesiastical Theology*. Translated by Kelley McCarthy Spoerl and Markus Vinzent. Fathers of the Church 135. Washington, DC: Catholic University of America Press, 2017.

Falluomini, Carla. *The Gothic Version of the Gospels and Pauline Epistles: Cultural Background, Transmission and Character*. Arbeiten zur Neutestamentlichen Textforschung 46. Berlin: De Gruyter, 2015.

Ferguson, Thomas C. *The Past is Prologue: The Revolution of Nicene Historiography*. Supplements to Vigiliae Christianae 75. Leiden: Brill, 2005.

Finazzi, Rosa Bianca, and Paola Tornaghi. "Gothica bononiensia: A New Document Under Linguistic and Philological Analysis." *Interdisciplinary Journal for Germanic Linguistics and Semiotic Analysis* 19, no. 2 (2014): 1–56.

Gassman, Mattias. "An Ancient Account of Pagan Origins: Making Sense of Filastrius, *Diuersarum hereseon liber* 111." *Revue d'études augustiniennes et patristiques* 67, no. 1 (2021): 83–105.

Gibbon, Edward. *The History of the Decline and Fall of the Roman Empire*, vol. 3. London: W. Strahan and T. Cadell, 1783.

Graumann, Thomas. "The Synod of Constantinople, AD 383: History and Historiography." *Millenium* 7, no. 1 (2010): 133–68.

Greatrex, Geoffrey. "Theodore Lector and the Arians of Constantinople." In *Studies in Theodore Anagnostes*, edited by Rafał Kosiński and Adrian Szopa, 207–31. Studi e testi tardoantichi 19. Brepols: Tournhout, 2021.

Gregg, Robert C., ed., *Arianism: Historical and Theological Reassessments, Papers from The Ninth International Conference on Patristic Studies, September 5–10, 1983, Oxford, England*. Patristic Monograph Series 11. Philadelphia: Philadelphia Patristic Foundation, 1985.

Gregg, Robert C., and Dennis E. Groh. *Early Arianism: A View of Salvation*. Philadelphia: Fortress Press, 1981.

Grillmeier, Aloys. *Christ in Christian Tradition*, vol. 1, *From the Apostolic Age to Chalcedon (451)*. Translated by John Bowden. 2nd ed. London: Mowbray, 1975.

Gryson, Roger. *Les palimpsestes ariens latins de Bobbio: Contribution à la méthodologie de l'étude des palimpsestes*. Armarium Codicum Insignium 2. Turnhout: Brepols, 1983.

———. *Scolies ariennes sur le concile d'Aquilée*. Sources chrétiennes 267. Paris: Éditions du Cerf, 1980.

———. "Les sermons ariens du *Codex latinus monacensis 6329*: Étude critique." *Revue des Études Augustiniennes* 39, no. 2 (1993): 333–58.

Gwynn, David M. *The Eusebians: The Polemic of Athanasius of Alexandria and the Construction of the "Arian Controversy."* Oxford Theological Monographs. Oxford: Oxford University Press, 2007.

Hagedorn, Dieter. *Der Hiobkommenter des Arianers Julian*. Patristische Texte und Studien 14. Berlin: De Gruyter, 1973.

Hänel, Gustav. *Lex Romana Visigothorum*. Berlin: Wilhelm Besser, 1849.

Hanson, R.P.C. "The Arian Doctrine of the Incarnation." In Gregg, ed., *Arianism*, 181–211.

———. *The Search for the Christian Doctrine of God: The Arian Controversy, 318–381*. Edinburgh: T&T Clark, 1988.

———. Who Taught ἐξ οὐκ ὄντων?" In Gregg, ed., *Arianism*, 79–83.

Haykin, Michael A.G. *The Spirit of God: The Exegesis of 1 and 2 Corinthians in the Pneumatomachian Controversy of the Fourth Century*. Supplements to Vigiliae Christianae. Leiden: Brill, 1994.

Heather, Peter. "The Crossing of the Danube and the Gothic Conversion." *Greek, Roman and Byzantine Studies* 27, no. 3 (1986): 289–318.

———. *Goths and Romans, 332–489*. Oxford Historical Monographs (Oxford: Oxford University Press, 1994).

Heather, Peter, and John Matthews. *The Goths in the Fourth Century*. Translated Texts for Historians 11. Liverpool: Liverpool University Press, 1991.

Heil, Uta, ed. *Athanasius von Alexandrien, De sententia Dionysii: Einleitung, Übersetzung und Kommentar*. Patristische Texte und Studien 52. Berlin: De Gruyter, 1999.

———. *Avitus von Vienne und die homöische Kirche der Burgunder*. Patristische Texte und Studien 66. Berlin: De Gruyter, 2011.

———. "The Homoians." In Berndt and Steinacher, eds., *Arianism*, 85–115.

*Hilary of Poitiers: Conflicts of Conscience and Law in the Fourth-Century Church.* Translated with introduction and notes by Lionel R. Wickham. Translated Texts for Historians 25. Liverpool: Liverpool University Press, 1997.

*Incomplete Commentary on Matthew (Opus imperfectum).* Translated by James A. Kellerman. Edited by Thomas C. Oden. 2 vols. Ancient Christian Texts. Downers Grove, IL: IVP Academic, 2010.

Johnson, Aaron P. "Narrating the Council: Eusebius on Nicaea." In *The Cambridge Companion to the Council of Nicaea*, edited by Young Richard Kim, 202–22. Cambridge: Cambridge University Press, 2021.

Karfíková, Lenka, Scot Douglass, Johannes Zachhuber, Johan Leemans, Matthieu Cassin, and Miguel Brugarolas, eds. *Gregory of Nyssa: Contra Eunomium, An English Version with Supporting Studies.* 3 vols. Supplements to Vigiliae Christianae 82, 124, 148. Leiden: Brill, 2007–18.

Kinzig, Wolfram. *A History of Early Christian Creeds.* Berlin: De Gruyter, 2024.

Kopecek, Thomas A. *A History of Neo-Arianism.* 2 vols. Patristic Monograph Series 8. Philadelphia: Philadelphia Patristic Foundation, 1979.

Korobov, Maksim, and Andrey Vinogradov, "Gotische Graffito-Inschriften aus der Bergkrim." *Zeitschrift für deutsches Altertum und deutsche Literatur* 145 (2016): 141–57.

Langworthy, Oliver B. *Gregory of Nazianzus' Soteriological Pneumatology.* Studien und Texte zu Antike und Christentum 117. Tübingen: Mohr Siebeck, 2019.

Lenski, Noel. "The Gothic Civil War and the Date of the Gothic Conversion." *Greek, Roman and Byzantine Studies* 36, no. 1 (1995): 51–87.

*The Letters of Saint Athanasius Concerning the Holy Spirit.* Translated by C.R.B. Shapland. London: Epworth Press, 1951.

Lienhard, Joseph T. *Contra Marcellum: Marcellus of Ancyra and Fourth-Century Theology.* Washington, DC: Catholic University of America Press, 1999.

Löhr, Winrich. "Arius Reconsidered (Part 2)." *Zeitschrift für Antikes Christentum* 10, no. 1 (2006): 121–57.

———. "A Sense of Tradition: The Homoiousian Church Party." In Barnes and Williams, eds., *Arianism after Arius*, 81–100.

Luibheid, Colm. "The Arianism of Eusebius of Nicomedia." *Irish Theological Quarterly* 43, no. 1 (1976): 3–23.

Martin, Annick. "Athanase et les néo-ariens." In Meyer, ed., *Philostorge*, 275–88.

Maspero, Giulio. "The Fire, the Kingdom and the Glory: The Creator Spirit and the Intra-Trinitarian Processions in the *Adversus Macedonianos* of Gregory of Nyssa." In *Gregory of Nyssa: The Minor Treatises on Trintiarian Theology and Apollinarianism*, edited by Volker Henning Drecoll and Margitta Berghaus, 229–76. Supplements to Vigiliae Christianae 106. Leiden: Brill, 2011.

Mathisen, R.W. "Sigisvult the Patrician, Maximinus the Arian, and Political Strategems in the Western Roman Empire, *c.* 425–40." *Early Medieval Europe* 8, no. 2 (1999): 173–96.

McConnell, Timothy P. *Illumination in Basil of Caesarea's Doctrine of the Holy Spirit.* Minneapolis, MN: Fortress Press, 2017.

McGuckin, John. *St. Gregory of Nazianzus: An Intellectual Biography.* Crestwood, NY: St. Vladimir's Seminary Press, 2001.

McLynn, Neil. *Ambrose of Milan: Church and Court in a Christian Capital.* Transformation of the Classical Heritage 22. Berkeley: University of California Press, 1994.

———. "The 'Apology' of Palladius: Nature and Purpose." *Journal of Theological Studies,* n.s., 42, no. 1 (1991): 52–76.

———. "From Palladius to Maximinus: Passing the Arian Torch." *Journal of Early Christian Studies* 4, no. 4 (1996): 477–93.

———. "Little Wolf in the Big City: Ulfila and His Interpreters." In *Wolf Liebeschuetz Reflected: Essays Presented by Colleagues, Friends and Pupils,* edited by John Drinkwater and Benet Salway, 125–35. Bulletin of the Institute of Classical Studies Supplement 91. London: Institute of Classical Studies, 2007.

Menze, Volker, "Ariminian Churches in the Germanic Kingdoms." In David G. Hunter , L.J. Lietaert Peerbolte, and Paul van Geest eds., *Brill Encyclopedia of Early Christianity.* Leiden: Brill, forthcoming.

Meslin, Michel. *Les Ariens d'occident, 335–430.* Patristica Sorbonensia 8. Paris: Éditions du Seuil, 1967.

Meyer, Doris, ed., with Bruno Bleckmann, Alain Chauvot, and Jean-Marc Prieur. *Philostorge et l'historiographie de l'Antiquité tardive.* Collegium Beatus Rhenanus 3. Stuttgart: Franz Steiner, 2011.

Morales, Xavier. "Identification de l'auteur des citations néo-ariennes dans le *Traité* de Basile d'Ancyre." *Zeitschrift für Antikes Christentum* 11, no. 3 (2008): 492–99.

Nautin, Pierre. "L''Opus imperfectum in Mattheum' et les Ariens de Constantinople." *Revue d'Histoire Ecclésiastique* 67, no. 2 (1972): 381–408.

*The Panarion of Epiphanius of Salamis, Book I (Sects 1–46).* Translated by Frank Williams. 2nd ed. Nag Hammadi and Manichaean Studies 63. Leiden: Brill, 2009.

*The Panarion of Epiphanius of Salamis, Books II and III. De fide.* Translated by Frank Williams. 2nd ed. Nag Hammadi and Manichaean Studies 79. Leiden: Brill, 2013.

Parvis, Sara. *Marcellus of Ancyra and the Lost Years of the Arian Controversy 325–345.* Oxford Early Christian Studies. Oxford: Oxford University Press, 2006.

———. "Was Ulfila Really a Homoian?" In Berndt and Steinacher, eds., *Arianism*, 49–65.

Prestige, G.L. *God in Patristic Thought.* London: SPCK, 1952.

Quasten, Johannes. *Patrology*, vols. 1–3. Utrecht: Spectrum, 1949–1960.

Radde-Gallwitz, Andrew. *Basil of Caesarea, Gregory of Nyssa, and the Transformation of Divine Simplicity.* Oxford Early Christian Studies. Oxford: Oxford University Press, 2009.

Ratkus, Artūras. "Greek ἀρχιερεύς in Gothic Translation: Linguistics and Theology at a Crossroads." *NOWELE* 71, no. 1 (2018): 3–34.

Ritter, Adolf Martin. "Arius redivivus? Ein Jahrzwölft Arianismusforschung." *Theologische Rundschau*, n.s., 55, no. 2 (1990): 153–87.

———. "Councils and Synods." In *The Brill Dictionary of Gregory of Nyssa*, edited by Lucas Francisco Mateo-Seco and Giulio Maspero, 180–82. Supplements to Vigiliae Christianae 99. Boston: Brill, 2010.

*Saint Basile: Lettres.* Edited and translated by Yves Courtonne. Vol. 3. Collection Budé. Paris: Belles Lettres, 1966.

Schäferdiek, Knut. "Das gotische liturgische Kalendarfragment: Bruchstück eines Konstantinopeler Martyrologs." *Zeitschrift für Neutestamentliche Wissenschaft* 79 (1988): 116–37. Reprinted in Schäferdiek, *Schwellenzeit*, 147–68.

———. *Schwellenzeit: Beiträge zur Geschichte des Christentums in Spätantike und Frühmittelalter*, edited by Winrich A. Löhr and Hanns Christof Brennecke. Arbeiten zur Kirchengeschichte 64. Berlin: De Gruyter, 1996.

———. "Theodor von Herakleia (328/34–351/55): Ein wenig bekannter Kirchenpolitiker und Exeget des vierten Jahrhunderts." *Romanitas–Christianitas: Untersuchungen zur Geschichte und Literatur der römischen Kaiserzeit, Johannes Sträub zum 70. Geburtstag am 18. Oktober 1982*, ed. Gerhard Wirth, with Karl-Heinz Schwarte and Johannes Heinrichs (Berlin: De Gruyter, 1982), 393–410. Reprinted in Schäferdiek, *Schwellenzeit*, 51–68.

Schlatter, Fredric W. "The Pelagianism of the Opus Imperfectum in Matthaeum." *Vigiliae Christianae* 41, no. 3 (1987): 267–84.

Siecienski, Edward. *The Filioque: History of a Doctrinal Controversy*. Oxford: Oxford University Press, 2010.

Simonetti, Manlio. "Arianesimo latino." *Studi Medievali*, 3rd s., 8, no. 2 (1967): 663–744.

———. *La crisi ariana nel IV secolo*. Studia Ephemeridis "Augustinianum" 11 (Rome: Institutum Patristicum "Augustinianum," 1975).

———. "Note di cristologia pneumatica." *Augustinianum* 12, no. 2 (1972): 201–32.

Smulders, Pierre. *La doctrine trinitaire de s. Hilaire de Poitiers*. Rome: Universitas Gregoriana, 1944.

Stead, G.C. "Divine Substance in Tertullian." *Journal of Theological Studies*, n.s., 14, no. 1 (1963): 46–66.

Steinhauser, Kenneth B. "The Acts of the Council of Aquileia (381 C.E.)." In *Religions of Late Antiquity in Practice*, edited by Richard Valantasis, 275–88. Princeton Readings in Religions. Princeton: Princeton University Press, 2000.

Sumruld, William A. *Augustine and the Arians: The Bishop of Hippo's Encounters with Ulfilan Arianism*. Selinsgrove, PA: Susquehanna University Press, 1994.

Szada, Marta. *Conversion and the Contest of Creeds in Early Medieval Christianity*. Cambridge: Cambridge University Press, 2024.

———. "The Missing Link: The Homoian Church in the Danubian Provinces and Its Role in the Conversion of the Goths." *Zeitschrift für Antikes Christentum* 24, no. 3 (2020): 549–84.

Teske, Roland J. trans. *Arianism and Other Heresies*. The Works of St. Augustine I/18. Hyde Park, NY: New City Press, 1995.

Thompson, E.A. *The Visigoths in the Time of Ulfila*. Oxford: Clarendon Press, 1966.

Toom, Tarmo. "Ulfila's Creedal Statement and Its Theology." *Journal of Early Christian Studies* 29, no. 4 (2021): 525–52.

Vaggione, Richard Paul. *Eunomius of Cyzicus and the Nicene Revolution*. Oxford Early Christian Studies. Oxford: Oxford University Press, 2000.

———. *Eunomius: The Extant Works*. Oxford Early Christian Texts. Oxford: Clarendon Press, 1987.

Van Nuffelen, Peter. "Considérations sur l'anonyme homéen." In *Les historiens fragmentaires de la langue grecque à l'époque romaine impériale et tardive*, edited by Eugenio Amato, Pasqua De Cicco, Bertrand Lançon, Tiphaine Moreau, 207–22. Rennes: Presses Universitaires de Rennes, 2021.

———. "Isolement et apocalypse: Philostorge et les eunomiens sous Théodose II." In Meyer, ed., *Philostorge*, 307–28.

Ward-Perkins, Bryan. "Where is the Archaeology and Iconography of Germanic Arianism?" In *Religious Diversity in Late Antiquity*, edited by David M. Gwynn and Susanne Bangert, 265–89. Late Antique Archaeology 6. Leiden: Brill, 2010.

Whelan, Robin. *Being Christian in Vandal Africa: The Politics of Orthodoxy in the Post-Imperial West*. Transformation of the Classical Heritage 59. Oakland: University of California Press, 2018.

Wickham, Lionel R. "The *Syntagmation* of Aetius the Anomean." *Journal of Theological Studies,* n.s., 19, no. 2 (1968): 532–69.

Wiles, Maurice. *Archetypal Heresy: Arianism Through the Centuries*. Oxford: Oxford University Press, 1996.

Williams, Daniel H. *Ambrose of Milan and the End of the Arian-Nicene Conflicts*. Oxford Early Christian Studies. Oxford: Clarendon Press, 1995.

———. "Another Exception to Later Fourth-Century 'Arian' Typologies: The Case of Germinius of Sirmium." *Journal of Early Christian Studies* 4, no. 3 (1996): 335–57.

Williams, Michael Stuart. *The Politics of Heresy in Ambrose of Milan: Community and Consensus in Late Antique Christianity*. Cambridge: Cambridge University Press, 2017.

Williams, Rowan. *Arius: Heresy and Tradition*, rev. ed. Grand Rapids, MI: Eerdmans, 2001.

———. "Baptism and the Arian Controversy." In Barnes and Williams, *Arianism after Arius*, 149–80.

Winn, Robert E. *Eusebius of Emesa: Church and Theology in the Mid-Fourth Century*. Washington, DC: Catholic University of America Press, 2011.

Wolfe, Brendan. "The Gothic Palimpsest of Bologna." *Studia Patristica* 92 (2017): 205–8.

———. "The Skeireins: a neglected text." *Studia Patristica* 64 (2013): 127–132.

Wolfe, Brendan, and Mattias Gassman. "'A Thing Like God': Re-Reading Gothic Philippians 2.6–8." *New Testament Studies* (forthcoming).

# ANNOTATED INDEX OF ANCIENT PEOPLE

# INDEX